PRESIDENTS

A Pictorial Guide
to the Presidents Birthplaces,
Homes, and Burial Sites

By
Rachel M. Kochmann

Photographs in this book were taken by the author and her husband, C.O. (Clancy) Kochmann, on a motor trip throughout the United States while visiting these historical sites of the presidents.

Presidential portraits courtesy of the Bureau of Engraving and Printing.

This book is dedicated to the people who mow the grass, maintain the roads and care for these historic sites, so that we may have a beautiful place to go to reflect on the thoughts and deeds of those who have given some of their years to lead and guide the United States of America.

Printed by James Barry Printing, Prescott, Arizona 86301

Presidential Flag

United States Flag

Presidents of the United States

UNITED STATES CAPITOL

This magnificent structure houses the Legislative Branch of our government and is the most visited building in Washington, D.C. Every four years a person, who has been elected by the people, comes to the steps of the east front of the capitol for his inauguration as President of the United States of America. Each President will try to govern the people to the best of his ability. Some men are well remembered and others are almost forgotten, but all have done something for their country.

THE WHITE HOUSE

This official home of the President of the United States stands on a site chosen by the first president, George Washington, himself. When a new President of the U.S. moves into the White House he enters a dwelling that is home, office and public show place, all in one. He heads a civil government and is commander-in-chief of the U.S. military forces. Callers from all over the world have found hospitality at the White House. Several of the rooms are open to the public. Many Americans feel that the White House is the symbol home of the nation itself.

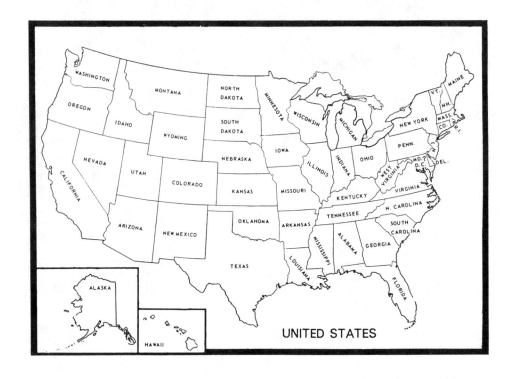

UNITED STATES

Presidential Birthplaces

Eight birthplaces are located in Virginia:

George Washington	Thomas Jefferson
James Madison	James Monroe
William H. Harrison	John Tyler
Zachory Taylor	Woodrow Wilson

Seven birthplaces are located in Ohio:

Ulysses S. Grant	Rutherford B. Hayes
James A. Garfield	Benjamin Harrison
William McKinley	William H. Taft
Warren G. Harding	

Four birthplaces are located in New York:

Martin Van Buren	Millard Fillmore
Theodore Roosevelt	Franklin D. Roosevelt

Three birthplaces are located in Massachusetts:

John Adams	John Quincy Adams
John F. Kennedy	

Two birthplaces are located in North Carolina:

James K. Polk	Andrew Johnson

Two birthplaces are located in Vermont:

Chester A. Arthur	Calvin Coolidge

Two birthplaces are located in Texas:

Dwight D. Eisenhower	Lyndon B. Johnson

One birthplace is located in each of the following:
- South Carolina: Andrew Jackson
- New Hampshire: Franklin Pierce
- Pennsylvania: James Buchanan
- Kentucky: Abraham Lincoln
- New Jersey: Grover Cleveland
- Iowa: Herbert Hoover
- Missouri: Harry S. Truman
- California: Richard M. Nixon
- Nebraska: Gerald R. Ford
- Georgia: James E. Carter
- Illinois: Ronald Reagan

Presidential Burial Sites

Seven burial sites are located in Virginia:

George Washington	Thomas Jefferson
James Madison	James Monroe
John Tyler	William H. Taft
John F. Kennedy	

Six burial sites are located in New York:

Martin Van Buren	Millard Fillmore
Ulysses S. Grant	Theodore Roosevelt
Franklin D. Roosevelt	Chester A. Arthur

Five burial sites are located in Ohio:

William H. Harrison	Rutherford B. Hayes
James A. Garfield	William McKinley
Warren G. Harding	

Three burial sites are located in Tennessee:

Andrew Jackson	James K. Polk
Andrew Johnson	

Two burial sites are located in Massachusetts:

John Adams	John Quincy Adams

One burial site is located in each of the following:
- Kentucky: Zachory Taylor
- Pennsylvania: James Buchanan
- New Hampshire: Franklin Pierce
- Illinois: Abraham Lincoln
- New Jersey: Grover Cleveland
- Indiana: Benjamin Harrison
- Washington, D.C.: Woodrow Wilson
- Vermont: Calvin Coolidge
- Iowa: Herbert C. Hoover
- Missouri: Harry S. Truman
- Kansas: Dwight D. Eisenhower
- Texas: Lyndon B. Johnson

GEORGE WASHINGTON

1st President

Term - April 30, 1789 to March 4, 1797

Federalist Party

Birth: Pope's Creek (Wakefield) Westmoreland County, Virginia, February 22, 1732.

Zodiac Sign: Pisces

Ancestry: English

Father: Augustine Washington. Born: Westmoreland County Virginia 1694. Died: King George County, Virginia April 12,1743.

Mother: Mary Ball Washington. Born: Lancaster County, Virginia 1708. Died: Near Fredericksburg, Virginia April 25, 1789.

Brothers: Samuel (1734 - 1781). John Augustine (1736 - 1787). Charles (1738 - 1799).

Sisters: Elizebeth (1733 - 1797). Mildred (1739 - 1740).

Half Brothers: Lawrence (1718 - 1752). Augustine (1720 - 1735).

Half Sisters: Jane (1722 - 1735).

Wife: Martha Dandridge Custis. Born: New Kent County Virginia June 21, 1731. Died: Mount Vernon, Virginia May 22, 1802. Buried: Mount Vernon, Virginia.

Marriage: Kent County, Virginia January 6, 1759.

Children: None (adopted two children from his wife's first marriage).

Home: Mount Vernon, Virginia

Education: Private tutoring by family.

Religion: Episcopalian

Occupation Before Presidency: Surveyor, soldier, planter.

Military Service: Virginia Militia (1752 - 1758). Commander in Chief of Continental Army (1775 - 1783).

Pre - Presidential Offices: Member of Virginia House of Burgesses Justice of Fairfax County, Delegate to First and Second Continental Congresses, President of Constitutional Convention.

Political Party: Favored Federalists

Age of Inauguration: 57

Election of 1789
(each elector voted for two men)

Candidates	Electoral Vote
George Washington	69
John Adams	34
John Jay	9
Nine Others	26

First Administration
President: George Washington
Vice President: John Adams - of Massachusetts
Inauguration: April 30, 1789
Federal Hall, New York City, New York

Election of 1792
(each elector voted for two men)

Candidates	Electoral Vote
George Washington	132
John Adams	77
George Clinton	50
Two Others	5

Second Administration
President: George Washington
Vice President: John Adams of Massachusetts
Inauguration: March 4, 1793
Federal Hall, Philadelphia, Pennsylvania

Occupation After Presidency: Planter and General of the Army.

President at Time of Death: John Adams

Death: Mount Vernon, December 14, 1799

Cause of Death: Pneumonia at age 67.

Place of Burial: Mount Vernon, Virginia.

"Let us raise a standard to which the wise and honest can repair; the rest is in the hands of God."
— Address to the Constitutional Convention, 1787

GEORGE WASHINGTON'S BIRTHPLACE
"POPES CREEK" (now) "WAKEFIELD," VIRGINIA

GEORGE WASHINGTON'S BOYHOOD HOME
"FERRY FARM" (NEAR) FREDERICKSBURG, VIRGINIA

George, first child of Augustine and Mary Ball Washington was born February 22, 1732 (new style calendar), at his father's estate, "Pope's Creek", on the west shore of the Potomic River.

The original house burned (1779) and was never rebuilt. This Memorial House now "Wakefield" was constructed during 1930 - 1931 as a memorial to George Washington. The building represents a typical home of the upper classes of the period. It has four rooms and a central hallway on each floor. The bricks were hand made from the clay of a nearby field. The house and the furnishings illustrate the setting into which George Washington was born and the manner of life his father led as a moderately wealthy planter in 18th century Tidewater, Virginia.

Uncovering the past, Archeological searches for physical remains at the George Washington birth place site have gone on since the latter part of the 19th century. Five structures have been located so far: the birthplace, the smoke house, the kitchen and two unidentified structures.

Oyster shells outline the plantation's main house, which was the building in which George Washington was born. It was a large, u-shaped building of at least nine rooms. These foundations have been covered over to preserve them.

When John Washington, Georges great-grandfather settled in the "Bridges Creek" area, he established a family burying ground near his house. Through the years, many of the Washingtons who lived at that home overlooking Popes Creek, were buried here. Thirty-two burials have been found at this location including those of George's half brother, father, grandfather and great grandfather. Two of the original gravestones remain.

Park facilities include the historic mansion area, colonial farm, burying ground, hiking trails and picnic area.

Location:

38 miles south east of Fredericksburg, Virginia on V.A. 3, then 2 miles east on V.A. 204.

Visit this farm where stories of George Washingtons youth abound; barking the cherry tree; throwing a dollar across the river; teaching himself surveying; and riding his fathers ferry to school each day.

Location:

712 King Highway, 1 mile east across Rappahannock River on V.A. 3, Fredericksburg, Virginia.

VIRGINIA

• GEORGE WASHINGTON'S BIRTHPLACE
POPES CREEK (now) WAKEFIELD, VIRGINIA

**MARY WASHINGTON'S HOUSE
FREDERICKSBURG, VIRGINIA**

George Washington bought this house for his mother in 1772. It was here he came to say goodby before leaving for New York and his inauguration. Mrs. Washington did not see her son again. She died in this house in 1789. At the rear of the house is the quarter-kitchen.

The English garden is excellent, and some of the boxwood planted by Mary Washington still remain.

Location:
   1201 Charles Street, Fredericksburg, Virginia.

**MARY WASHINGTON MONUMENT AND GRAVE
FREDERICKSBURG, VIRGINIA**

This shaft, dedicated by President Grover Cleveland in 1894, marks the burial place of George Washington's mother, Mary Ball Washington. On these grounds she used to read to her grandchildren, the Lewises of Kenmore, as they sat on the over-look ever since called Meditation Rock.

Location:
   On Washington Avenue, Fredericksburg, Virginia.

GEORGE WASHINGTON'S HOME
"MT. VERNON", VIRGINIA

GEORGE WASHINGTON'S BURIAL SITE
"MT. VERNON", VIRGINIA

George Washington brought his gracious and beautiful bride here in 1759 and with characteristic and ingenious industry began his plan to become the leading scientific farmer in America. He kept elaborate notes, conferred with many farmers, tried crop rotation, and other new experiments, added to his stately Georgian Colonial Mansion and planned for the family which nature unhappily denied him. He and his wife brought up two of her children by a previous marriage and adopted two of her grandchildren.

The nucleus of the existing house was built before 1735 by Augustine Washington, George's father. George inherited it after the death of his half-brother, Lawrence, in 1752.

Family, home and farm became the focal point of Washington's life. But he was a great patriot as well as a brilliant planner. And when he was called to lead the armies of the country he loved, he did not hesitate. When he had won freedom for his fellow Americans he returned, determined to live as he wished. But four years later he was called to preside at the Constitutional Convention in Philadelphia and in 1789 became the first president. From 1797 until his death on December 14, 1799 he lived again at "Mount Vernon", he and his wife Martha are buried here.

Location:

Mount Vernon is located at the southern terminus of the Mount Vernon Memorial Highway, 8 miles south of Alexandria, Virginia, and 16 miles from downtown Washington, D.C.

On Saturday, December 14, 1799, George Washington suffering from a tracheal infection (possibly tuberculosis), prepared to pay "the dept which we all must pay."

"I am not afraid to go", he said, just before he died he put the fingers of his left hand on his right wrist and counted his pulse, his lips moving.

A few months before his death General Washington selected this site for a new family burial vault and included in his will directions for its construction. His executors did not comply with his directive until 1831. The marble sarcophagus was provided in 1831. The outer and enclosing wall were added at that time.

On a stone tablet above the vault gate, the modest inscription, "Within this Enclosure Rests the remains of Genl. George Washington", suggests silence and respect.

The old vault, a short distance east of the new site has been restored and retained.

Location:

Mount Vernon is located at the southern terminus of the Mount Vernon Memorial Highway, 8 miles south of Alexandria, Virginia, and 16 miles from downtown Washington, D.C.

VIRGINIA

GEORGE WASHINGTON'S BURIAL SITE
■ **"MT. VERNON", VIRGINIA**

4

JOHN ADAMS
2nd President

**Term - March 4, 1797
to March 4, 1801**

Federalist Party

John Adams

Birth: Braintree (Quincy), Massachusetts October 30, 1735.

Zodiac Sign: Scorpio

Ancestry: English

Father: John Adams. Born: Braintree (Quincy) Massachusetts January 28, 1691. Died: Braintree (Quincy) Massachusetts May 25, 1761.

Mother: Susanna Boylston Adams. Born: Brookline, Massachusetts March 5, 1699. Died: Braintree (Quincy) Massachusetts April 17, 1797.

Brothers: Peter Boylston (1738 - 1823). Elihu (1741 - 1775).

Wife: Abigail Smith. Born: Weymouth, Massachusetts November 11, 1744. Died: Quincy, Massachusetts October 28, 1818. Buried: First Parish Church, Quincy, Massachusetts.

Marriage: Weymouth, Massachusetts October 25, 1764.

Children: Abigail Amelia (1765 - 1813). John Quincy (1767 - 1848). Susanna (1768 - 1770). Charles (1770 - 1800). Thomas Boylston (1772 - 1832).

Home: Peacefield, Quincy, Massachusetts.

Education: Attended private schools in Braintree; received B.A. (1755) and M.A. (1758) from Harvard.

Religion: Unitarian

Occupation Before Presidency: Teacher, farmer, lawyer.

Pre - Presidential Offices: Representative to Massachusetts General Court; Delegate to First and Second Continental Congresses; Member of Provincial Congress of Massachusetts; Delegate to Massachusetts Constitutional Convention; Commissioner to France; Minister to Netherlands and England; Vice President.

Political Party: Federalist

Age of Inauguration: 61

Election of 1789
(each elector voted for two men)

Candidates	Electoral Vote
John Adams (Federalist)	71
Thomas Jefferson (Democratic - Republican)	68
Thomas Pinckney (Federalist)	59
Aaron Burr (Democratic - Republican)	30
Samuel Adams (Democratic - Republican)	15
Oliver - Ellsworth (Federalist)	11
Seven Others	22

The Adams Administration

President: John Adams

Vice President: Thomas Jefferson of Virginia

Inauguration: March 4, 1797

Federal Hall, Philadelphia, Pennsylvania

Occupation After Presidency: Writer

President at Time of Death: John Quincy Adams

Death: Quincy, Massachuttes July 4, 1826.

Cause of Death: Debility at age 90.

Place of Burial: First Unitarian Church, Quincy, Massachusetts.

"Liberty cannot be preserved without a general knowledge among the people."
— Dissertation on the Canon and Feudal Law, 1765

JOHN ADAMS' BIRTHPLACE
BRAINTREE (now) QUINCY, MASSACHUSETTS

JOHN ADAMS' HOME
"PEACEFIELD" QUINCY, MASSACHUSETTS

John Adams, first Vice - President and second - President of the United States was born on October 19, 1735, "The Cradle of American Independence," his birthplace, was built in 1681. He graduated from Harvard College in 1755, and was admitted to the bar in 1758. He took a keen interest in town affairs and wrote on public matters for the newspaper.

Abigail Adams wrote most of her famous letters to her husband, John Adams, while he was serving in the Continental Congress in Philadelphia and as an arbitrator for peace in Paris.

The John Adams birthplace remained in possession of the Adams family until 1940, when it was deeded to the city of Quincy. In 1963 the birthplace was officially designated as a Registered National Landmark by the United States Government.

Location:
133 Franklin Street, Quincy, Massachusetts.

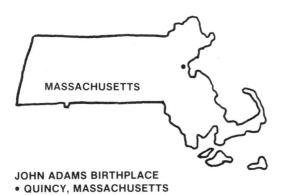

JOHN ADAMS BIRTHPLACE
• QUINCY, MASSACHUSETTS

JOHN ADAMS' HOME
"PEACEFIELD" QUINCY, MASSACHUSETTS

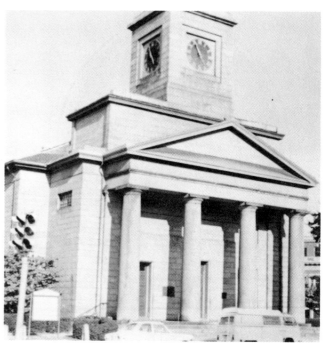

JOHN ADAMS' BURIAL SITE
FIRST PARISH CHURCH, QUINCY, MASSACHUSETTS

One of America's most distinguished families, the Adams family (four generations) lived in this Georgian Clapboard house, called "Peacefield" by John Adams. Later generations called the house the "Old House". John Adams bought the house in 1787 while he was minister to Great Britain. He added several rooms the next year and then moved in.

The Adams Family presented this site in 1946 to the United States Government for the American people. This beautiful home with its priceless heirlooms and many fine examples of Colonial furniture and furnishings, contributed by the Adams Family, the garden, the stone library, and the carriage house are open to the public.

Location:

135 Adams Street, Quincy, Massachusetts.

John Adams died at age ninety on appropriately, the Fourth of July, 1826, the fiftieth anniversary of the Declaration of Independence. His last words were "Jefferson still survives". But Jefferson in fact did not. He had died at Monticello several hours earlier.

Within this edifice of classical architecture and austere simplicity, built of Quincy granite in 1828 are the tombs of John Adams and his wife Abilgail.

The Adams crypt is the only location in the United States where two President's and their wives are buried side by side. (John Adams and his wife Abilgail and John Quincy Adams and his wife Louisa Catherine). The crypt is located in the basement of the church which has come to be known as the Adams Temple.

Location:

1306 Hancock Street, Quincy, Massachusetts.

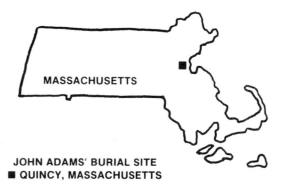

MASSACHUSETTS

JOHN ADAMS' BURIAL SITE
■ **QUINCY, MASSACHUSETTS**

THOMAS JEFFERSON
3rd President

Term - March 4, 1801
to March 4, 1809

Democratic - Republican Party

Birth: "Shadwell", Goochland (now Albemarle) County, Virginia, April 13, 1743.

Zodiac Sign: Aries

Ancestry: Welsh

Father: Peter Jefferson. Born: Chesterfield County, Virginia February 29, 1708. Died: "Shadwell", Virginia August 17, 1757.

Mother: Jane Randolph Jefferson. Born: London, England February 9, 1720. Died: "Shadwell", Virginia March 31, 1776.

Brother: Randolph (1755 - 1815).

Sisters: Jane (1740 - 1765). Mary (1741 - 1760). Martha (1746 - 1811). Lucy (1752 - 1784). Anna Scott (1755 - ?).

Wife: Martha Wayles Skelton. Born: Charles City, County, Virginia October 19, 1748. Died: "Monticello", Virginia September 6, 1782. Buried: "Monticello", Virginia.

Marriage: "The Forest" Charles City, County, Virginia January 1, 1772

Children: Martha (1772 - 1836). Maria (1778 - 1804). Lucy Elizabeth (1782 - 1785). (two daughters and a son died in infancy)

Home: "Monticello", Charlottesville, Virginia

Education: Private tutoring; Attended country school in Albermarle County, Virginia; Received B.A. from College of William and Mary.

Religion: No specific denomination

Occupation Before Presidency: Planter, lawyer, writer, philosopher, scientist, architect.

Pre-Presidential Offices: Member of Virginia House of Burgesses; County Lieutenant; County Surveyor; Deputy Delegate to Second Continental Congress; Member of Virginia House of Delegates; Governor of Virginia; Commissioner to France; Minister to France; Secretary of State; Vice President.

Political Party: Democratic - Republican
Age at Inauguration: 57
Election of 1800
(Each elector voted for two men. A tie between Jefferson and Burr resulted, and the House of Representatives elected Jefferson President.)

Candidates	Electoral Vote
Thomas Jefferson (Democratic - Republican)	73
Aaron Burr (Democratic - Republican)	73
John Adams (Federalist)	65
Charles C. Pinckney (Federalist)	64
John Jay (Federalist)	1

First Administration
President: Thomas Jefferson
Vice President: Aaron Burr of New York
Inauguration: March 4, 1801
Senate Chambers, Washington D.C.

Election of 1804
(The Twelfth Amendment, ratified in September, 1804 provided for separate voting for President and Vice President, and precluded a repetition of the Jefferson - Burr tie of 1800.)

Candidates	Electoral Vote
Thomas Jefferson (Democratic - Republican)	162
Charles C. Pinckney (Federalist)	14

Second Administration
President: Thomas Jefferson
Vice President: George Clinton of New York
Inauguration: March 4, 1805
Senate Chamber, Washington D.C.

Occupation After Presidency: Planter, writer, educator.

President at Time of Death: John Quincy Adams

Death: "Monticello", Charlottesville, Virginia, July 4, 1826

Cause of Death: Diarrhea at age 83.

Place of Burial: "Monticello", Charlottesville, Virginia.

"If there by any among us who would wish to dissolve this Union or to change its republican form, let them stand undisturbed as monuments of the safety with which error of opinion may be tolerated when reason is left free to combat it."

— Inaugural Address, 1801

**THOMAS JEFFERSON'S BIRTHPLACE
"SHADWELL," CHARLOTTESVILLE, VIRGINIA**

Thomas Jefferson's father, Peter Jefferson acquired the land in 1735, and built the house about 1737. Thomas Jefferson was born here April 13, 1743. He lived here, 1743-1745, and 1752-1770. The house burned in 1770, and Jefferson then moved to Monticello.

Location:

This Historical Marker is located a few miles east of Charlottesville, Virginia on U.S. Hwy. 250.

**THOMAS JEFFERSON'S BOYHOOD HOME
"TUCKAHOE" (near) RICHMOND, VIRGINIA**

Tuckahoe, situated along the James River, was the boyhood home of Thomas Jefferson for 7 years and the place where he obtained his elementary education. The mansion, outbuildings, and surrounding gardens and lands constitute an outstanding example of a southern plantation.

Location:

About 13 miles west of Richmond, Virginia on V.A. 650.

A private residence, not open to the public.

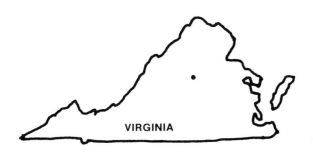

**THOMAS JEFFERSON'S BIRTHPLACE
• "SHADWELL" CHARLOTTESVILLE, VIRGINIA**

THOMAS JEFFERSON'S HOME
"MONTICELLO" (near) CHARLOTTESVILLE, VIRGINIA

"Monticello", one of the handsomest estates in Virginia, considered a classic of American Architecture, the house was designed and built by Jefferson on a land grant made to his father. Starting in 1769, he built with painstaking care, using materials made on the spot even to the nails. When his father's house "Shadwell" burned in 1771, Jefferson moved into the first completed outbuildings of his new home. A year later he brought his bride Martha Wayles Skelton here. It was not until 1809 that the main house was finally completed.

The house is of the classic examples of American Architecture. It is a three story building of thirty-five rooms including twelve in the basement. The dominating feature is the dome which commands the garden or west front. The room under the dome, octagonal in shape, is often referred to as the ballroom, however Mr. Jefferson always referred to it as the sky room.

Location:
3 miles south west of Charlottesville, Virginia on V.A. 53.

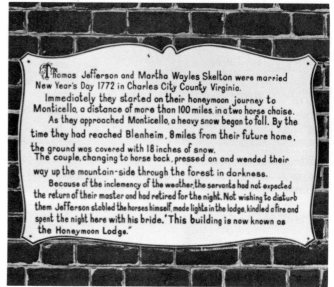

THOMAS JEFFERSON'S "HONEYMOON LODGE"
"MONTICELLO" (near) CHARLOTTESVILLE, VIRGINIA

Thomas Jefferson and Martha Wayles Skelton were married New Year's Day 1772 in Charles City County, Virginia.

Immediately they started on their honeymoon journey to Monticello, a distance of more than 100 miles, in a two horse chaise.

As they approached Monticello, a heavy snow began to fall. By the time they had reached Blenheim, 8 miles from their future home, the ground was covered with 18 inches of snow.

The couple, changing to horse back, pressed on and wended their way up the mountain-side through the forest in darkness.

Because of the inclemency of the weather, the servants had not expected the return of their master and had retired for the night. Not wishing to disturb them, Jefferson stabled the horses himself, made lights in the lodge, kindled a fire and spent the night here with his bride. "This building is now known as the Honeymoon Lodge."

Location:
3 miles S.E. of Charlottesville, Virginia on V.A. 53.

THOMAS JEFFERSON'S RETREAT
"POPLAR FOREST", LYNCHBURG, VIRGINIA

THOMAS JEFFERSON'S BURIAL SITE
"MONTICELLO" (near) CHARLOTTESVILLE, VIRGINIA

On July 4, 1826, the fiftieth anniversary of the Declaration of Independence, the third President of the United States died a few hours before his friend, John Adams.

Thomas Jefferson lies buried in the family graveyard which he laid out on the mountain side adjacent to the road leading from the house to the lodge. Title to this plot has never left the family, for when the estate was sold in 1831, title was retained. It is now maintained by the Monticello Association, an organization of the descendants of Jefferson, whose members have a right of burial there.

In his account book in 1826, Jefferson wrote these instructions for the inscription to be cut on his tombstone, and sketched the "plain die or cube — surmounted by an obelisk" he wanted on his grave. He did not note that he had been President of the United States, but wished "most to be remembered" for founding the University of Virginia, and for writing the Declaration of Independence and Virginia's Act for Religious Freedom. The last line should read: Died July 4, 1826.

Location:

3 miles S.E. of Charlottesville, Virginia on V.A. 53.

THOMAS JEFFERSON'S RETREAT
"POPLAR FOREST", LYNCHBURG, VIRGINIA

In 1806 - 1819 Thomas Jefferson designed and built "Poplar Forest", a notable octagonal house on his 4000 acre Bedford County Plantation as a summer home and retreat. He occupied it itermittently until his death in 1826.

Location:

About 6½ miles west of Lynchburg, Virginia on county route 661.

A private residence not open to the public.

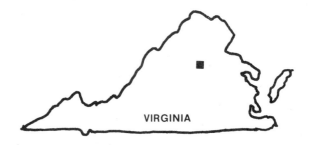

THOMAS JEFFERSON'S BURIAL SITE
■ "MONTICELLO" (near) CHARLOTTESVILLE, VIRGINIA

JAMES MADISON
4th President

Term - March 4, 1809 to March 4, 1817

Democratic - Republican Party

Birth: Port Conway, Virginia, March 16, 1751.

Zodiac Sign: Pisces

Ancestry: English

Father: James Madison. Born: March 27, 1723. Died: "Montpelier" Orange County, Virginia, February 27, 1801.

Mother: Eleanor Conway Madison. Born: Caroline County, Virginia, January 9, 1732. Died: "Montpelier" Orange County, Virginia, February 11, 1829.

Brothers: Francis (1753 - ?). Ambrose (1755 - 1793). William (1762 - 1843). Reuben (1771 - 1775).

Sisters: Nelly (1760 - 1802). Sarah (1761 - ?). Elizabeth (1768 - 1775). Francis (1771 - ?).

Wife: Dorothea (Dolley) Payne Todd. Born: Guilford County, North Carolina, May 20, 1768. Died: Washington D.C., July 12, 1849. Buried: "Montpelier", Virginia.

Marriage: "Harewood" Jefferson County, Virginia. September 15, 1794.

Children: None.

Home: "Montpelier", Virginia

Education: Received early education at Donald Robertson's school in Virginia and from private tutors; Awarded BA from the College of New Jersey (Princeton 1771), one year postgraduate study at Princeton.

Religion: Episcopalian

Occupation Before Presidency: Member of Orange County Committee of Safety; Delegate to the Virginia Convention; Member of Virginia Legislature; Member of Virginia Executive Council; Delegate to Continental Congress; Delegate to Annapolis Convention; Delegate to Constitutional Convention; Member of the Virginia Ratification Convention; U.S. Congressman; Secretary of State.

Age at Inauguration: 57

Election of 1808

Candidates	Electoral Vote
James Madison (Democratic - Republican)	122
Charles C. Pinckney (Federalist)	47
George Clinton (Independent - Republican)	6

First Administration
President: James Madison
Vice President: George Clinton of New York
Inauguration: March 4, 1809
House of Representatives, Washington D.C.

Election of 1812

Candidates	Electoral Vote
James Madison (Democratic - Republican)	128
DeWitt Clinton (Fusion)	89

Second Administration
President: James Madison
Vice President: Elbridge Gerry of Massachusetts
Inauguration: March 4, 1813
House of Representatives, Washington D.C.

President at Time of Death: Andrew Jackson

Death: "Montpelier", Virginia, June 28, 1836

Cause of Death: Debility at age 85.

Place of Burial: "Montpelier", Virginia.

"The public good, the real welfare of the great body of the people, is the supreme object to be pursued . . ."
— The Federalists, 1788

JAMES MADISON'S BIRTHPLACE
PORT CONWAY, VIRGINIA

DRIVE WAY TO "MONTPELIER"

At this place, "Port Conway", James Madison, fourth President of the United States and Father of the Constitution, was born March 16, 1751. His mother was staying at her paternal home, "Belle Grove", 400 yards east when her son was born. Madison's father, James Madison, Sr., lived in Orange County. The President had his home at Montpelier in that county.

Location:

4 miles north of Port Royal, Virginia on U.S. 301, or 12 miles south on the Rappahannock River.

JAMES MADISON HOME
"MONTPELIER" (near) ORANGE, VIRGINIA

"Montpelier", or "Montpellier", was James Madison's residence for nearly all his life. Born at his grandmother's home in King George County in 1751, he soon traveled with his mother to his father's farm, a tract in Orange County that had been in the family since 1723 and that became the nucleus of Montpelier. There, he first lived in a modest wooden house, constructed by his grandfather, Ambrose Madison, about two decades earlier and probably located a half mile south of the present mansion. The early, or central portion of the present Georgian residence was constructed by his father, also named James, about 1760. When the latter died in 1801, he bequeathed the house and part of the estate to his oldest son, James.

Location:

4 miles west of Orange, Virginia, 1 mile off Virginia 20.

Privately owned, the estate, except for the Madison family cemetery, is not open to the public.

VIRGINIA

• JAMES MADISON'S BIRTHPLACE
PORT CONWAY, VIRGINIA

13

JAMES MADISON'S HOME
"THE OCTAGON", WASHINGTON, D.C.

JAMES MADISON'S BURIAL SITE
"MONTPELIER" (near) ORANGE, VIRGINIA

JAMES MADISON'S HOME
"THE OCTAGON", WASHINGTON, D.C.

When the White House was burned by the British during the War of 1812, President and Mrs. James Madison (Dolly) were forced to live elsewhere while it was being rebuilt. They accepted the hospitality of Colonel John Tayloe, a wealthy Virginia planter, who offered them his unique 18th century Georgian townhouse known as The Octagon. The Madisons lived there for nearly a year in 1814 and 1815. They resided in a suite on the east side of the second floor, consisting of a large room and two small dressing rooms.

President Madison used the tower room above the house's entrance as a study, where on February 17, 1815, he signed the Treaty of Ghent, which ended the War of 1812.

Location:
1799 New York Ave. N.W. at 18th Street, Washington, D.C.

On June 27, 1836, James Madison spent several hours dictating a letter. The next morning breakfast was brought to him in bed, but he could not swallow. When his niece asked him what was wrong, he replied, "Nothing more than a change of (mind), my dear". And then according to his servant, James Madison "Ceased breathing as quietly as the snuff of a candle goes out".

James, and Dolley Madison are buried in a family plot near "Montpelier", Virginia. They had no children, but they reared the son of Mrs. Madison by her first husband.

Location:
4 miles west of Orange, Virginia and 1 mile off Virginia 20 — watch for sign Madison Graveyard.

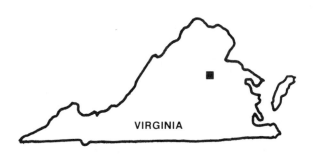

■ JAMES MADISON'S BURIAL SITE
"MONTPELIER" (near) ORANGE, VIRGINIA

JAMES MONROE
5th President

Term - March 4, 1817 to March 4, 1825

Democratic - Republican Party

James Monroe

Birth: Westmoreland County, Virginia. April 28, 1758.

Zodiac Sign: Taurus

Ancestry: Scotch

Father: Spence Monroe. Date of Birth (Unknown). Died: Westmoreland County, Virginia 1774.

Mother: Elizabeth Jones Monroe. Date of Birth (Unknown). Date of Death (Unknown).

Brothers: Andrew (Died 1826). Joseph Jones (Died 1824).

Wife: Elizabeth Kortright. Born: New York, New York, June 30, 1768. Died: Oak Hill, Virginia, September 23, 1830. Buried: Hollywood Cemetery, Richmond, Virginia.

Marriage: New York, New York. February 15, 1786.

Children: Eliza (1787 - ?). Maria Hester (1804 - 1850).

Homes: Ash Lawn, Charlottesville, Virginia. Oak Hill, Loudown County, Virginia.

Education: Parson Campbell's school; College of William and Mary.

Religion: Episcopalian

Occupation Before Presidency: Lawyer

Military Service: Officer in Third Virginia Regiment and Continental Army (1776 - 1779).

Pre-Presidential Offices: Military Commissioner for Southern Army; Rep. to Virginia Legislature; Member of Governor Jefferson's Council; Rep. to Virginia House of Delegates; Rep. to Continental Congress; Rep. to Virginia Assembly; Rep. to U.S. Senate; Minister to France; Minister to England; Governor of Virginia; Secretary of State; Secretary of War.

Age at Inauguration: 58

Election of 1816

Candidates	Electoral Vote
James Monroe (Democratic - Republican)	183
Rufus King (Federalist)	34

First Administration

President: James Monroe

Vice President: Daniel D. Tompkins of New York

Inauguration: March 4, 1817

The Capital, Washington, D.C.

Election of 1820

Candidates	Electoral Vote
James Monroe (Democratic - Republican)	231
John Quincy Adams (Independent - Republican)	1

Second Administration

President: James Monroe

Vice President: Daniel D. Tompkins of New York

Inauguration: March 5, 1821

House of Representatives, Washington, D.C.

Occupation After Presidency: Writer

President at Time of Death: Andrew Jackson

Death: New York, New York, July 4, 1831

Cause of Death: Debility at age 73.

Place of Burial: Hollywood Cemetery, Richmond, Virginia.

"The American continents . . . are henceforth not to be considered as subjects for future colonization by any European powers."

— Monroe Doctrine, 1823

JAMES MONROE'S BIRTHPLACE
(near) COLONIAL BEACH, VIRGINIA

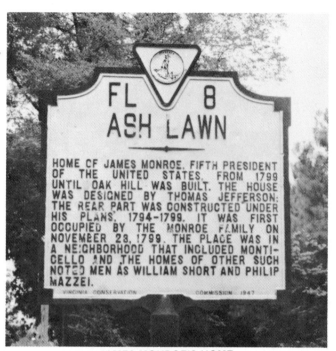

JAMES MONROE'S HOME
"ASH LAWN" (near) CHARLOTTESVILLE, VIRGINIA

James Monroe was born in Westmoreland County, Virginia on April 28, 1758. His father, Colonel Spence Monroe, came from a Scottish family that settled in Virginia in the mid-1600's. The family of his mother, Elizabeth Jones Monroe, came from Wales, and also had lived in Virginia for many years.

James studied at home with a tutor until he was 12 years old. Then his father sent him to the school of Parson Archibold Campbell. The boy had to leave home early in the morning and tramped miles through the forest to reach Campbell's school. He often carried a rifle and shot gun on the way. At the age of 16, James entered the College of William and Mary, but the stirring events of the Revolutionary War soon lured him into the army.

Monroe's birthplace, near Colonial Beach, Virginia fell into ruin, and no one knows exactly what the building looked like.

Location:

Between Oak Grove, Virginia and Colonial Beach, Virginia on V.A. 205.

JAMES MONROE'S HOME
"ASH LAWN" (near) CHARLOTTESVILLE, VIRGINIA

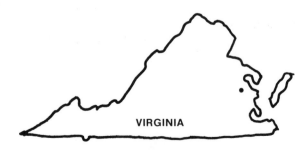

VIRGINIA

• JAMES MONROE'S BIRTHPLACE
(near) COLONIAL BEACH, VIRGINIA

JAMES MONROE'S HOME
"ASH LAWN" (near) CHARLOTTESVILLE, VIRGINIA

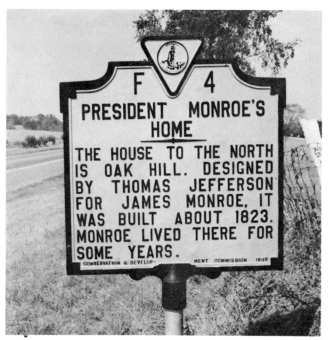

JAMES MONROE'S HOME
"OAK HILL" (near) LEESBURG, VIRGINIA

This 600 acre estate then called "Highland" planned by Thomas Jefferson for his friend, James Monroe was built in 1798. Monroe moved into the almost completed home on November 23, 1799. It was from here that he left to become the fifth President of the United States in 1817.

"Ash Lawn" has become known for its boxwood garden, at one time believed to have been designed after gardens which Monroe had seen while serving as United States Minister to France.

A focal point of the garden is the noted statue of Monroe which was created by sculptor Attilio Piccirilli. Originally sculpted for a South American government in honor of the Monroe Doctrine, the statue was presented to "Ash Lawn" by the sculptor.

Location:

5 miles south east of Charlottsville, Virginia on County Road 795, or 2½ miles beyond "Monticello", Thomas Jefferson's estate.

DRIVE WAY TO "OAK HILL"
JAMES MONROE'S HOME
"OAK HILL" (near) LEESBURG, VIRGINIA

17

**JAMES MONROE'S HOME
"OAK HILL" (near) LEESBURG, VIRGINIA**

James Monroe began building this palatial mansion at the height of his career, during his first term as President (1817 - 1821), drafted the Monroe Doctrine in it, and retired there at the end of his public service.

Spending much time at "Oak Hill", Monroe made horseback trips to and from the capital. On the grounds, among numerous locust and poplar trees, he planted an oak for each State in the Union, and thereby gave the estate its name.

In 1825, James Monroe left the White House and retired at "Oak Hill". He served for five years as a regent of the University of Virginia. In 1829, he became presiding officer of the Virginia Constitutional Convention. His wife died on September 23, 1830 and was buried at "Oak Hill". Late in 1830, he moved to New York City to live with his daughter and her husband.

Location:

Loudown County, Virginia. On U.S. 15, about 1 mile north of its junction with U.S. 50 at Gilbert's Corner, and about 8 miles south of Leesburg, Virginia.

Privately owned, is not open to the public.

JAMES MONORE'S BURIAL SITE
HOLLYWOOD CEMETERY, RICHMOND, VIRGINIA

This tomb contains the remains of President James Monroe. Upon his death in New York City on July 4, 1831, his body was interred in that city's Marble (Second Street) Cemetery. In 1858, the 100th Anniversary of his birth, municipal officials and representatives of the State of Virginia decided that the remains should be returned to his home state for reburial, at Hollywood Cemetery in Richmond, Virginia.

Hollywood Cemetery, on a rolling ridge overlooking the James River, also contains the graves of President John Tyler, and Jefferson Davis, President of the Confederate States of America.

Location:
412 South Cherry Street, Richmond, Virginia.

JAMES MONROE LAW OFFICE MUSEUM
AN MEMORIAL LIBRARY
FREDERICKSBURG, VIRGINIA

President James Monroe's long public career began in this building in 1786. Today, it houses a large and beautiful collection of the personal possessions of the President, including furniture, portraits, china, silver, jewelry, and porcelains used by the Monroes in the White House, 1817 to 1825, and the desk with its secret compartments on which he signed the Monroe Doctrine.

Location:
908 Charles Street, Fredericksburg, Virginia

VIRGINIA

■ **JAMES MONROE'S BURIAL SITE**
HOLLYWOOD CEMETERY, RICHMOND, VIRGINIA

JOHN QUINCY ADAMS
6th President

Term - March 4, 1825
to March 4, 1829

Democratic - Republican Party

John Quincy Adams.

Birth: Baintree (Quincy), Massachusetts. July 11, 1767
Zodiac Sign: Cancer
Ancestry: English
Father: John Adams. Born: Braintree (Quincy), Massachusetts, October 30, 1735. Died: Quincy, Massachusetts, July 4, 1826.
Mother: Abigail Smith Adams. Born: Weymouth, Massachusetts, November 11, 1744. Died: Quincy, Massachusetts, October 28, 1818.
Brothers: Charles (1770 - 1800). Thomas Boylston (1772 - 1832).
Sisters: Abigail Amelia (1776 - 1813). Susanna (1768 - 1770).
Wife: Louisa Catherine Johnson. Born: London, England, February 12 1775. Died: Washington, D.C., May 14, 1852. Buried: First Parish Church, Quincy, Massachusetts.
Marriage: London, England. July 26, 1797.
Children: George Washington (1801 - 1829). John (1803 - 1834). Charles Francis (1807 - 1886). Louisa Catherine (1811 - 1812).
Education: Studied in Paris, Amsterdam, Leyden, and The Hague; received B.A. (1787) from Harvard; studied law (1788 - 1790) with Theophilus Parsons.
Religion: Unitarian
Occupation Before Presidency: Lawyer, professor.
Pre-Presidential Offices: Minister to the Netherlands; Minister to Prussia; Member of Massachusetts Senate; Member of U.S. Senate; Minister to Russia; Minister to Great Britain; Secretary of State.
Political Party: Federalist to 1808; Democratic - Republican to 1825; National Republican (Whig) thereafter.
Age at Inauguration: 57

Election of 1824
(Although Jackson received more votes that Adams, no candidate had a majority, so the election was submitted to the House of Representatives, which chose Adams.)

Candidates	Electoral Vote
Andrew Jackson	99
John Quincy Adams	84
William H. Crawford	41
Henry Clay	37

The Adams Administration
President: John Quincy Adams
Vice President: John Calhoun of South Carolina
Inauguration: March 4, 1825
Hall of the House of Representatives, Washington, D.C.

Occupation After Presidency: Congressman, writer.
President at Time of Death: James Knox Polk
Death: Washington, D.C., February 23, 1848
Cause of Death: Paralysis at age 80.
Place of Burial: First Unitarian Church, Quincy, Massachusetts.

"The great object of the institution of civil government is the improvement of the condition of those who are party to the social compact . . ."
— Message to Congress, 1825

**JOHN QUINCY ADAMS' BIRTHPLACE
QUINCY, MASSACHUSETTS**

John Quincy Adams was born on July 11, 1767, in the family home in Braintree (now Quincy), Massachusetts. He was the second child and eldest son of the second President of the United States.

The Birthplace of President John Quincy Adams was built in 1767. Here was written the Constitution of the Commonwealth of Massachusetts in 1779 which was used as the model for the Constitution of the United States.

Location:

141 Franklin Street, Quincy, Massachusetts.

**ADAMS NATIONAL HISTORIC SITE
QUINCY, MASSACHUSETTS**

**• JOHN QUINCY ADAMS' BIRTHPLACE
QUINCY, MASSACHUSETTS**

One of America's most distinguished families, the Adams' family (four generations) lived in the Georgian clapboard house, called "Peacefield" by John Adams. Later generations called the house the "Old House". John Adams bought the house in 1787 while he was minister to Great Britain. He added several rooms the next year and then moved in.

The Adams Family presented this site in 1946 to the United States Government for the American people. This beautiful home with its priceless hierlooms and many fine examples of Colonial furniture and furnishings, contributed by the Adams Family, the garden, the stone library, and the carriage house are open to the public.

Location:

135 Adams Street, Quincy, Massachusetts.

JOHN QUINCY ADAMS' BURIAL SITE
FIRST PARISH CHURCH, QUINCY MASSACHUSETTS

John Quincy Adams suffered a paralytic stroke in 1846, but he recovered and returned to Congress. On February 21, 1848, he suffered another stroke at his House desk. Too ill to be moved from the building, he was carried to the Speaker's room. He died there two days later. His final words were: "This is the last of earth. I am content." Adams was buried in the churchyard of the First Unitarian Church of Quincy, Massachusetts.

Within this edifice of classical architecture and austere simplicity, built of Quincy granite in 1828 are the tombs of John Quincy Adams and his wife, Louisa Catherine.

The Adams crypt is the only location in the United States where two Presidents and their wives are buried side by side. John Adams and his wife Abigail and John Quincy Adams and his wife Louisa Catherine. The crypt is located in the church which has come to be known as the Adams Temple.

Location:

1306 Hancock Street, Quincy, Massachusetts.

■ **JOHN QUINCY ADAMS' BURIAL SITE**
FIRST PARISH CHURCH, QUINCY, MASSACHUSETTS

Andrew Jackson (signature)

ANDREW JACKSON
7th President

Term - March 4, 1829 to March 4, 1837

Democratic Party

Birth: "The Waxhaws", South Carolina. March 15, 1767

Zodiac Sign: Pisces

Ancestry: Scotch - Irish

Father: Andrew Jackson. Born: Ireland. Died: Waxhaws, South Carolina, early March, 1767.

Mother: Elizabeth Hutchinson Jackson. Born: Ireland. Died: Charleston, South Carolina, November, 1781.

Brothers: Hugh (1762 - 1780). Robert (1765 - 1780).

Wife: Rachel Donelson Robards. Born: Halifax County, Virginia, June 15, 1767. Died: Nashville, Tennessee, December 22, 1828. Buried: "The Hermitage", Tennessee.

Marriage: Natchez, Mississippi. August 1, 1791.

Second Ceremony: Nashville, Tennessee. January 17, 1794.

Children: Andrew Jackson, Jr. (adopted) (1810 - ?).

Home: "The Hermitage", Nashville, Tennessee

Education: Attended public school, studied law in Salisbury, South Carolina.

Religion: Presbyterian

Occupation Before Presidency: Lawyer, soldier, politician.

Military Service: Judge advocate of Davidson County Militia (c. 1791); Major general of Tennessee Militia (1802 - 1812); Major general of U.S. Army (1814 - 1821).

Pre-Presidential Offices: Attorney General of Western District of North Carolina; Delegate to Tennessee State Constitutional Convention; Member of U.S. House of Representatives; Member of U.S. Senate; Tennessee Supreme Court Judge; Governor of Florida Territory.

Age at Inauguration: 61

Election of 1828

Candidates	Electoral Vote
Andrew Jackson (Democratic)	178
John Quincy Adams (National Republican)	83

First Administration

President: Andrew Jackson

Vice President: John Calhoun of South Carolina (resigned December 28, 1832)

Inauguration: March 4, 1829

The Capital, Washington, D.C.

Election of 1832

Candidates	Electoral Vote
Andrew Jackson (Democratic)	219
Henry Clay (National Republican)	49
John Floyd (Nullifier)	11
William Wirt (Antimasonic)	7

Second Administration

President: Andrew Jackson

Vice President: Martin Van Buren of New York

Inauguration: March 4, 1833

House of Representatives, Washington, D.C.

President at Time of Death: James Knox Polk

Death: "The Hermitage", Nashville, Tennessee. June 8, 1845

Cause of Death: Consumption, dropsy at age 78.

Place of Burial: "The Hermitage", Nashville, Tennessve.

"There are no necessary evils in government. Its evils exist only in its abuses. If it would confine itself to equal protection, and, as Heaven does its rain, shower its favors alike on the high and low, the rich and poor, it would be an unqualified blessing."

— Veto of the Bank Renewal Bill, 1832

ANDREW JACKSON'S BIRTHPLACE
WAXHAW, SOUTH CAROLINA

Andrew Jackson, American soldier and statesman, 7th President of the United States, was born on March 15, 1767, at the Waxhaw settlement in either South Carolina or North Carolina — no one really knows which. Jackson believed he was born on the farm of his uncle, James Crawford near Waxhaw settlement, South Carolina. The Crawford house stood on the west side of the road that formed the boundary between North Carolina and South Carolina at that time.

Location:
14 miles south of Rock Hill, South Carolina on S.C. 5.

ANDREW JACKSON HISTORIC PARK
(near) LANCASTER, SOUTH CAROLINA

This State Park is named for Andrew Jackson, who was born about 100 yards north of the park museum building. Here stood the home of James Crawford and his wife Jane. The Crawford home offered refuge to Elizabeth Hutchinson Jackson, sister of Jane, where she journeyed from 12 mile creek a few days after the death of her husband to give birth to her third son. Thus there was born on the eve of the Revolution, a boy who destined to become President of the United States and one of the most colorful figures in the annals of our history.

Location:
10 miles north of Lancaster, South Carolina on U.S. Hwy. 521.

SOUTH CAROLINA

• ANDREW JACKSON'S BIRTH PLACE
WAXHAW, SOUTH CAROLINA

**ANDREW JACKSON'S BURIAL SITE
"THE HERMITAGE", NASHVILLE, TENNESSEE**

On June 8, 1845, Andrew Jackson fell unconscious. When he awakened, he saw his weeping slaves crowded about him. "Oh, do not cry." Jackson told them. "Be good children and we will all meet in heaven." Jackson died that evening.

This tomb is located in a picturesque corner of the garden, still guarded by hickory trees planted from a parcel of hickory nuts sent to Jackson in 1830. President Jackson chose to be buried here next to his beloved wife, Rachel, near the home and grounds he loved.

In the stillness of the Hermitage garden, a visitor who stops to reflect on the greatness of Andrew Jackson can almost hear the music of the fife and drum, the shouted battle command. He can almost catch a fluting glimpse of a tall, erect figure leading his men into battle. The heritage of Jackson is the heritage of America.

Location:
12 miles east of Nashville, Tennessee off I-40 to Hickory Exit.

**ANDREW JACKSON'S HOME
"THE HERMITAGE", NASHVILLE, TENNESSEE**

The Hermitage, one of the nation's most widely visited national shrines, is nestled in the rolling middle Tennessee hills.

The 625 acres on which the Hermitage stands were originally purchased by Andrew Jackson in 1804. The first mansion was built in 1819 and was extensively remodeled in 1831 while Jackson was President. Heavily damaged by fire in 1834, the Hermitage was rebuilt with the original walls and foundation being retained. The mansion and farm are preserved today much as they were in Jackson's time.

The Mansion with its beautiful white pillars, its wide verandas, spacious front hall and graceful spiral staircase, is a fine example of Pre-Civil War southern colonial architecture.

Paintings, crystal, mirrors, kitchen utensils, are all there much as they were when Jackson lived. The furnishings belong to the Jackson family.

Location:
12 miles east of Nashville, Tennessee off I-40 to Hickory Exit.

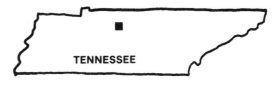

**■ ANDREW JACKSON'S BURIAL SITE
"THE HERMITAGE", NASHVILLE, TENNESSEE**

25

MARTIN VAN BUREN
8th President

Term - March 4, 1837 to March 4, 1841

Democratic Party

Birth: Kinderhook, New York. December 5, 1782.
Zodiac Sign: Sagittarius
Ancestry: Dutch
Father: Abraham Van Buren. Born: Albany, New York, February 17, 1737. Died: Kinderhook, New York, April 8, 1817.
Mother: Maria Hoes Van Alen Van Buren. Born: February 27, 1747. Died: Kinderhook, New York, February 16, 1817.
Brothers: Lawrence (1786 - 1868). Abraham (1788 - 1836).
Sisters: Derike (1777 - 1865). Hannah (1780 - ?).
Half Brother: James Isaac Van Alen (1776 - 1870).
Wife: Hannah Hoes. Born: Kinderhook, New York, March 8, 1783. Died: Albany, New York, February 5, 1819. Buried: Kinderhook Cemetery, Kinderhook, New York.
Marraige: Catskill, New York, February 21, 1807.
Children: Abraham (1807 - 1873). John (1810 - 1866). Martin (1812 - 1855). Smith Thompson (1817 - 1876).
Home: "Lindenwald", Kinderhook, New York
Education: Village schools, studied in law office.
Religion: Dutch Reformed
Occupation Before Presidency: Lawyer, politician.
Pre-Presidential Offices: Surrogate of Columbia County, New York; New York State Senator; Attorney General of New York; Delegate to Third New York State Constitutional Convention; U.S. Senator; Governor of New York; Secretary of State; Vice President of the United States.
Political Party: Democratic during Presidency; Free - Soil from 1848.
Age at Inauguration: 54

Election of 1836

Candidates	Electoral Vote
Martin Van Buren (Democratic)	170
William H. Harrison (Whig)	73
Hugh L. White (Whig)	26
Daniel Webster (Whig)	14
Willie P. Mangum (Anti-Jacksonian)	11

The Van Buren Administration
President: Martin Van Buren
Vice President: Richard M. Johnson of Kentucky
Inauguration: March 4, 1837
The Capital, Washington, D.C.
Occupation After Presidency: Politician
President at Time of Death: Abraham Lincoln
Death: Kinderhook, New York. July 24, 1862
Cause of Death: Asthma at age 79.
Place of Burial: Kinderhook Cemetery, Kinderhook, New York.

"From a small community we have risen to a people powerful in numbers and strength; but with our increase has gone hand in hand the progress of just principles."
— Inaugural Address, 1837

MARTIN VAN BUREN'S BIRTHPLACE
KINDERHOOK, NEW YORK

Martin Van Buren was born December 5, 1782 at 46 Hudson Street in the Dutch Community of Kinderhook, New York. His father, who had fought in the war for Independence, won his livelihood as a tavern keeper and farmer. Martin Van Buren attended village schools for several years. At the age of 14 he read law with a local attorney, but soon moved to New York City to pursue his legal studies.

The house has been torn down.

Location:

William Street and Hudson Street, Kinderhook, New York.

MARTIN VAN BUREN'S HOME
"LINDENWALD", KINDERHOOK, NEW YORK

Martin Van Buren, who had been born and raised in Kinderhook, New York, decided in 1839, during his Presidency, to retire in the area. That same year, he purchased the Van Ness house and about 130 acres of land. By 1845, he had acquired 90 more acres. Meantime, 4 years earlier, after his defeat for a second term, he retired to the residence, which he named "Lindenwald" after the linden groves on the property. He died there in 1862 and was buried in Kinderhook Cemetery.

The exterior of "Lindenwald" is being restored.

Location:

3 miles south of Kinderhook, New York on Route 9H.

NEW YORK

• MARTIN VAN BUREN'S BIRTHPLACE
KINDERHOOK, NEW YORK

27

**MARTIN VAN BUREN'S BURIAL SITE
KINDERHOOK CEMETERY, KINDERHOOK, NEW YORK**

Plagued by asthma for many months, Martin Van Buren died at "Lindenwald" on July 24, 1862, and was buried beside his wife, Hannah, in Kinderhook Cemetery, Kinderhook, New York.

Location:

24 miles south of Albany, New York on Hwy. 9, west of Kinderhook, New York.

NEW YORK

■ **MARTIN VAN BUREN'S BURIAL SITE
KINDERHOOK, NEW YORK**

WILLIAM-HENRY-HARRISON
9th President

Term - March 4, 1841
to April 4, 1841

Whig Party

Birth: "Berkeley Plantation", Charles City County, Virginia. February 9, 1773

Zodiac Sign: Aquarius

Ancestry: English

Father: Benjamin Harrison. Born: Charles City County, Virginia, April 5, 1726. Died: Charles City County, Virginia, April 24, 1791.

Mother: Elizabeth Bassett Harrison. Born: Eltham estate, Charles City County, Virginia, December 13, 1730. Died: Charles City County, Virginia, 1792.

Brothers: Benjamin (1755 - 1799). Carter Bassett (? - 1808).

Sisters: Elizabeth (1751 - ?). Ann (1753 - 1821). Lucy (? - 1809). Sarah (1770 - 1812).

Wife: Anna Tuthill Symmes. Born: Morristown, New Jersey, July 25, 1775. Died: North Bend, Ohio, February 25, 1864. Buried: William Henry Harrison State Park, North Bend, Ohio.

Marraige: North Bend, Ohio. November 25, 1795.

Children: Elizabeth Bassett (1796 - 1846). John Cleves Symmes (1798 - 1830). Lucy Singleton (1800 - 1826). William Henry (1802 - 1838). John Scott (1804 - 1878). Benjamin (1806 - 1840). Mary Symmes (1809 - 1842). Carter Bassett (1811 - 1839). Anna Tuthill (1813 - 1845). James Findlay (1814 - 1817).

Home: Grouseland, Vincennes, Indiana

Education: Private tutoring; attended Hampden Sidney College.

Religion: Episcopalian

Occupation Before Presidency: Soldier, politician

Military Service: U.S. Army (1791 - 1798), rose from ensign to captain; as governor of Indiana Territory, fought Indians at Tippecanoe (1811); commissioned major general of Kentucky Militia (1812); U.S. Army (1812 - 1814), rose from brigadier general to major general in command of the Northwest.

Pre-Presidential Offices: Secretary of Northwest Territory; U.S. Representative; Governor of Indiana Territory and Superintendent of Indian Affairs; Ohio State Senator; U.S. Senator; Minister to Colombia.

Age at Inauguration: 68

Election of 1840

Candidates	Electoral Vote
William Henry Harrison (Whig)	234
Martin Van Buren (Democratic)	60

The Harrison Administration

President: William Henry Harrison
Vice President: John Tyler of Virginia
Inauguration: March 4, 1841
The Capital, Washington, D.C.

Death: Washington, D.C., April 4, 1841

Cause of Death: Pleuresy, pneumonia at age 68.

Place of Burial: William Henry Harrison State Park, North Bend, Ohio.

"The only legitimate right to govern is an express of power from the governed."

— Inaugural Address, 1841

**WILLIAM HENRY HARRISON'S BIRTHPLACE
"BERKELEY", CHARLES CITY, VIRGINIA**

"Berkeley" has a distinction shared only with the Adams house in Massachusetts. It was the ancestral home of two Presidents, the birthplace of William Henry Harrison, our ninth President and the ancestral home of his grandson, Benjamin Harrison, our twenty-third President.

"Berkeley" is a beautiful, excellently restored example of the brick mansions that graced Virginia's "Golden Age". Built in 1726 by Benjamin Harrison, grandfather of William Henry Harrison, it is believed to be the oldest three story brick house in Virginia.

"Taps" was composed here in 1862. The first official Thanksgiving was held here in 1619.

Location:

On Scenic Route 5 between Williamsburg and Richmond, Virginia. 8 miles west of Charles City, Virginia.

**WILLIAM HENRY HARRISON'S BIRTHPLACE
"BERKELEY", CHARLES CITY, VIRGINIA**

William Henry Harrison was born on February 9, 1773, at "Berkeley", his father's plantation in Charles City County, Virginia.

William received his early education at home. He entered Hampden-Sydney College in 1787, but left before graduation because his father wanted him to study medicine. After his father died in 1791, Harrison dropped medicine and joined the army.

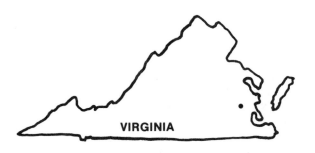

**• WILLIAM HENRY HARRISON'S BIRTHPLACE
"BERKELEY", CHARLES CITY, VIRGINIA**

30

WILLIAM HENRY HARRISON'S HOME
"GROUSELAND", VINCENNES, INDIANA

WILLIAM HENRY HARRISON'S BURIAL SITE
HARRISON TOME STATE MEMORIAL, NORTH BEND, OHIO

This mansion, now surrounded by the city of Vincennes, preserves the memory of William Henry Harrison, Indian fighter, military leader in the War of 1812, Governor of Indiana Territory, and ninth President of the United States. He built "Grouseland" and lived in it during most of his term as Territorial Governor, when he helped bring peace to the old northwest and opened to white settlement a vast territory between the Ohio River and the Great Lakes.

"Grouseland" is a 2½ story, brick Georgian house containing 26 rooms and 13 fireplaces. It resembles Berkeley, Harrison's birthplace and boyhood home in Virginia and may have been designed by him.

Location:

3 West Scott Street at Park, Vincennes, Indiana.

In 1840, William Henry Harrison was the Whig Party's candidate for President, and the famous "Log Cabin and Hard Cider" campaign, "Tippecanoe and Tyler too", swept him into office. "Old Tip" was by now 67 years old. The hardships of soldiering, the arduous political campaign, and now the harassment of insistent office-seekers undermined his rugged constitution. After only a month in office, the President died of pneumonia.

Harrison himself had expressed a desire to be buried on Mt. Nebo with its wide view of the beautiful Ohio River and the corners of three states, Ohio, Kentucky, and Indiana.

He was buried July 7, 1841, in an unostentatious tomb provided by his family on the summit of Mt. Nebo. The tomb itself remains essentially as it was last renovated by the Harrison family. Twenty-four vaults are provided within the tomb. They contain the bodies of President Harrison, his wife Anna, their son, John Scott, father of President Benjamin Harrison, and other members of the family. Several sealed vaults are unmarked.

Location:

17 miles south west of Cincinnati, Ohio on U.S. Hwy. 50. On Loop Avenue south of Harrison Avenue, North Bend, Ohio.

OHIO

■ WILLIAM HENRY HARRISON'S BURIAL SITE
HARRISON TOMB STATE MEMORIAL, NORTH BEND, OHIO

31

JOHN TYLER
10th President

Term - April 4, 1841 to March 4, 1845

Whig Party

John Tyler

Birth: "Greenway", Charles City County, Virginia. March 29, 1790.

Zodiac Sign: Aries

Ancestry: English

Father: John Tyler. Born: James City County, Virginia, February 28, 1747. Died: "Greenway", Charles City County, Virginia, January 6, 1813.

Mother: Mary Marot Armistead Tyler. Born: York County, Virginia, 1761. Died: "Greenway", Charles City County, Virginia, April 5, 1797.

Brothers: Wat Henry (1788 - 1862). William (? - 1856).

Sisters: Anne Contesse (1778 - 1803). Elizabeth Armistead (1780 - 1824). Martha Jefferson (1782 - 1855). Maria Henry (1784 - 1843). Christianna Booth (1795 - 1842).

First Wife: Letitia Christian. Born: Cedar Grove Plantation, New Kent County, Virginia, November 12, 1790. Died: White House, Washington, D.C., September 10, 1842. Buried: Cedar Grove Plantation, Kent County, Virginia.

First Marraige: "Cedar Grove" Plantation, New Kent County, Virginia. March 29, 1813.

Second Wife: Julia Gardiner. Born: Gardiner's Island, New York, May 4, 1820. Died: Richmond, Virginia, July 10, 1889. Buried: Hollywood Cemetery, Richmond, Virginia.

Second Marriage: New York, New York. June 26, 1844.

Children: (by first wife) Mary (1815 - 1848). Robert (1816 - 1877). John (1819 - 1896). Letitia (1821 - 1907). Elizabeth (1823 - 1850). Anne Contesse (1825 - 1825). Alice (1827 - 1854). Tazewell (1830 - 1874).

Children: (by second wife) David Gardiner (1846 - 1927). John Alexander (1848 - 1883). Julia (1849 - 1871). Lachlan (1851 - 1902). Lyon Gardiner (1853 - 1935). Robert Fitzwalter (1856 - 1927). Pearl (1860 - 1947).

Home: "Sherwood Forest", Charles City County, Virginia

Education: Local Virginia schools; graduated from College of William and Mary (1807).

Religion: Episcopalian

Occupation Before Presidency: Lawyer

Military Service: Captain of volunteer company in Richmond, Virginia (1813).

Pre-Presidential Offices: Member of Virginia House of Delegates; U.S. Representative; Governor of Virginia; U.S. Senator; Vice President of the U.S.

Age at Inauguration: 51

Note: The first vice president who succeeded to the presidency because of the death of his predecessor, William Henry Harrison.

The Tyler Administration
President: John Tyler
Inauguration: April 6, 1841
Indian Queen Hotel, Washington, D.C.

Occupation After Presidency: Lawyer

President at Time of Death: Abraham Lincoln

Death: Richmond, Virginia. January 18, 1862

Cause of Death: Bilious Fever at age 71.

Place of Burial: Hollywood Cemetery, Richmond, Virginia.

"The institutions under which we live, my countrymen, secure each person in the perfect enjoyment of all his rights."

— Inaugural Address, 1841

DRIVE TO GREENWAY
JOHN TYLER BIRTHPLACE
"GREENWAY", CHARLES CITY, VIRGINIA

John Tyler was born at "Greenway" Estate in Charles City County, Virginia on March 29, 1790. He was the second son of John and Mary Armistead Tyler.

Young John had a mind of his own. When only 11 years old, he led a revolt against his tyrannical schoolmaster, William McMurdo. His father sent him to William and Mary College in 1802. The boy studied hard and became especially interested in political subjects. He relaxed from his studies by writing poetry and playing the violin. John was graduated at the age of 17. He then studied law under his father, and was admitted to the Virginia bar in 1809.

The old law office which was used by both father and son, is still standing. The home, built in the last half of the 18th century was restored with care in the 1940's and is a fine example of the one and a half story frame houses of its period, retaining much of its interior paneling. It can be seen from Route 5 in Virginia.

Privately owned.

Location:

One mile south of Charles City, Virginia or 30 miles east of Richmond, Virginia or 20 miles west of Williamsburg, Virginia on Route 5.

JOHN TYLER'S BIRTHPLACE
"GREENWAY", CHARLES CITY, VIRGINIA

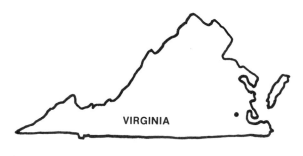

• JOHN TYLER'S BIRTHPLACE
"GREENWAY", CHARLES CITY, VIRGINIA

JOHN TYLER'S HOME
"SHERWOOD FOREST", (near) CHARLES CITY, VIRGINIA

JOHN TYLER'S HOME
"SHERWOOD FOREST" (near) CHARLES CITY, VIRGINIA

Sherwood Forest was the home of President John Tyler (1841 - 1845). Considered the longest frame house in America, it is 300 feet long. Built 1730, altered and renovated by President Tyler in 1844, the house looks very much as it did when Tyler retired from the White House in 1845, and brought with him to "Sherwood Forest" his bride of several months, the beautiful Julia Gardiner of Gardiner's Island, New York. Since this time, the plantation has been continuously occupied by members of the Tyler family, and has been a working plantation for over 240 years. All of the original 1600 acres are still in the Tyler name.

The house contains a private ballroom 68 feet in length, and is superbly furnished with family heirlooms of the 18th and 19th century. President Tyler's porcelain, china, silver, mirrors, girondoles, table, chairs, and other furnishings are still in use at "Sherwood Forest". In the library are the books of Governor Tyler (President Tyler's father), President Tyler, and President Tyler's son, Dr. Lyon Gardiner Tyler.

This estate originally called Creek Plantation, was named "Sherwood Forest" by President Tyler, who likened himself to Robin Hood, a political outlaw.
Location:
35 miles east of Richmond, 18 miles west of Williamsburg, Virginia.

34

**JOHN TYLER'S BURIAL SITE
HOLLYWOOD CEMETERY, RICHMOND, VIRGINIA**

John Tyler retired to "Sherwood Forest", his estate near Charles City, Virginia, and lived quietly until just before the Civil War. In February, 1861, he headed a southern peace mission to Washington seeking a compromise on the issues that threatened the Union. In April, at a Virginia secession convention, Tyler voted in favor of Virginia leaving the Union. He won election to the Confederate House of Representatives in November, 1861, but died on January 18, 1862, before taking his seat. In 1915, Congress dedicated a monument to Tyler's memory in Hollywood Cemetery at Richmond, Virginia, where he is buried beside his second wife, Julia.

Location:
   412 South Cherry Street, Richmond, Virginia.

VIRGINIA

■ **JOHN TYLER'S BURIAL SITE
HOLLYWOOD CEMETERY, RICHMOND, VIRGINIA**

JAMES K. POLK
11th President

**Term - March 4, 1845
to March 4, 1849**

Democratic Party

Birth: Mecklenburg County, North Carolina. November 2, 1795.

Zodiac Sign: Scorpio

Ancestry: Scotch - Irish

Father: Samuel Polk. Born: Tyron, North Carolina, July 5, 1772. Died: Columbia, Maury County, Tennessee, November 5, 1827.

Mother: Jane Knox Polk. Born: Iredell County, North Carolina, November 15, 1776. Died: Columbia, Maury County, Tennessee, January 11, 1852.

Brothers: Franklin Ezekiel (1802 - 1831). Marshall Tate (1805 - 1831). John Lee (1807 - 1831). William Hawkins (1815 - 1862). Samuel Wilson (1817 - 1839).

Sisters: Jane Maria (1798 - 1876). Lydia Eliza (1800 - 1864). Naomi Tate (1809 - 1836). Ophelia Clarissa (1812 - 1851).

Wife: Sarah Childress. Born: Murfreesboro, Tennessee, September 4, 1803. Died: Nashville, Tennessee, August 14, 1891. Buried: Capitol Hill, Nashville, Tennessee.

Marriage: Murfreesboro, Tennessee. January 1, 1824.

Children: None

Home: "Polk House", Columbia, Tennessee

Education: Private school; received B.A. from the University of North Carolina.

Religion: Presbyterian

Occupation Before Presidency: Lawyer

Pre-Presidential Offices: Member of Tennessee Legislature; U.S. Representative; Speaker of the House of Representatives; Governor of Tennessee.

Age at Inauguration: 49

Election of 1844

Candidates	Electoral Vote
James K. Polk (Democratic)	170
Henry Clay (Whig)	105
James G. Birney (Liberty)	—

The Polk Administration
President: James Polk
Vice President: George M. Dallas of Pennsylvania
Inauguration: March 4, 1845
The Capitol, Washington, D.C.

Occupation After Presidency: Retired

President at Time of Death: Zachary Taylor

Death: Nashville, Tennessee. June 15, 1849.

Cause of Death: Diarrhea at age 53.

Place of Burial: State Capitol Grounds, Nashville, Tennessee.

"We must ever maintain the principle that the people of this continent alone have the right to decide their own destiny."

— Message to Congress, 1845

JAMES K. POLK'S BIRTHPLACE
PINEVILLE, NORTH CAROLINA

The first dark horse in American presidential politics, James K. Polk was born in 1795 on the 250 acre farm worked by his parents, Jane and Samuel Polk.

James Polk spent most of his childhood among the gently rolling hills of Mecklenburg County.

Reconstruction of his birthplace includes a log cabin, various subsidiary buildings, and a visitor center museum. Furnishings in the house and kitchen date to years prior to 1806, when the Polks moved to Tennessee. A 30 minute movie depicts the eleventh president's career. Guided tours are offered of the restored log structures. A picnic area is located on the grounds.

Location:

½ mile south of Pineville, North Carolina on U.S. 521.

JAMES K. POLK'S BIRTHPLACE
PINEVILLE, NORTH CAROLINA

• JAMES K. POLK'S BIRTHPLACE
PINEVILLE, NORTH CAROLINA

37

**JAMES K. POLK'S ANCESTRAL HOME
COLUMBIA, TENNESSEE**

**JAMES K. POLK'S ANCESTRAL HOME
COLUMBIA, TENNESSEE**

The Polk home reflects the Polk way of life — tasteful, yet modest. Known for his honesty and integrity, he refused to accept gifts while serving as President. The furnishings are those used by the President and Mrs. Polk in the White House, items used by Polk in his law office and some of the furnishings used by the Samuel Polk family in the same house.

An especially rare item is the Inaugural Bible used by Polk. The large collection of outstanding portraits include the Presidential company portraits by G. P. A. Healy, and portraits by R. E. W. Earl of Congressman and Mrs. Polk.
Location:
 301 West 7th Street, Columbia, Tennessee.

JAMES K. POLK'S BURIAL SITE
STATE CAPITOL GROUNDS
NASHVILLE, TENNESSEE

After his successor, Zachory Taylor, was inaugurated, the white-haired Polk returned to his home in Nashville, Tennessee, worn out by four years of hard work. He became ill with cholera and died June 15, 1849. Polk was buried in the city cemetery, and later in the garden tomb east of his estate, "Polk Place". For a time, Mrs. Polk managed a plantation on the Yalobusha River. She died in 1891, and was buried beside her husband. In 1893, their tombs were moved to the grounds of the Tennessee Capitol in Nashville.

Location:

Sixth and Charlotte Avenue, Nashville, Tennessee.

The mortal remains of
JAMES KNOX POLK,
are resting in the vault beneath.
He was born in Mecklenburg County
North Carolina,
and emigrated with his father,
Samuel Polk, to Tennessee
in 1806.
The beauty of virtue
was illustrated in his life:
The excellence of Christianity
was exemplified in his death.

SARAH CHILDRESS
WIFE OF JAMES KNOX POLK
1803 ——— 1891

JAMES K. POLK'S BURIAL SITE
STATE CAPITOL GROUNDS
NASHVILLE, TENNESSEE

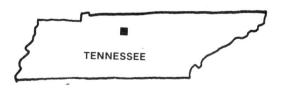

■ JAMES K. POLK'S BURIAL SITE
STATE CAPITOL GROUNDS
NASHVILLE, TENNESSEE

ZACHARY TAYLOR
12th President

**Term - March 4, 1849
to July 9, 1850**

Whig Party

Birth: "Montebello", Orange County, Virginia. November 24, 1784.

Zodiac Sign: Sagittarius

Ancestry: English

Father: Lt. Col. Richard Taylor. Born: Orange County, Virginia, April 3, 1744. Died: Near Louisville, Kentucky, January 19, 1829.

Mother: Sarah Dabney Strother Taylor. Born: December 14, 1760. Died: December 13, 1822.

Brothers: Hancock (1781 - 1841). William Dabney Strother (1782 - 1808). George (1790 - 1829). Joseph Pannill (1796 - 1864).

Sisters: Elizabeth Lee (1792 - 1845). Sarah Bailey (1799 - 1851). Emily Richard (1801 - 1841).

Wife: Margaret Mackall Smith. Born: Calvert County, Maryland, September 21, 1788. Died: Near Pascagoula, Mississippi, August 18, 1852. Buried: Zachary Taylor National Cemetery, Louisville, Kentucky.

Marriage: Jefferson County, Kentucky. June 21, 1810.

Children: Anna Mackall (1811 - 1875). Sarah Knox (1814 - 1835). Sarah married Jefferson Davis June 17, 1835. Place of Marriage: Lexington, Kentucky. Davis became President of the Confederate States of America in 1861. Octavia Pannill (1816 - 1820). Margaret Smith (1819 - 1820). Maly Elizabeth (1824 - 1909). Richard (1826 - 1879).

Education: Limited tutorial education.

Religion: Episcopalian

Occupation Before Presidency: Soldier; farmer.

Military Service: Volunteer in Kentucky Militia (1803); rose from first lieutenant to major general in U.S. Army (1808 - 1849).

Age at Inauguration: 64

Election of 1848

Candidates	Electoral Vote
Zachary Taylor (Whig)	163
Lewis Cass (Democratic)	127
Martin Van Buren (Free - Soil)	—

The Taylor Administration

President: Zachary Taylor
Vice President: Millard Fillmore of New York
Inauguration: March 5, 1849
The Capitol, Washington, D.C.

Death: Washington, D.C. July 9, 1850.

Cause of Death: Coronary thrombosis at age 65.

Place of Burial: Zachary Taylor National Cemetery, Louisville, Kentucky.

"For more than half a century . . . this Union has stood unshaken. Whatever dangers may threaten it, I shall stand by it and maintain it in its integrity to the full extent of the obligations imposed and the powers conferred upon me by the Constitution."

— Message to Congress, 1849

ZACHARY TAYLOR'S BIRTHPLACE
"MONTEBELLO", (near) BARBOURSVILLE, VIRGINIA

Zachary Taylor was born near Barboursville, Virginia on November 24, 1784. His parents, Richard and Sarah Strother Taylor, came from leading families of the Virginia plantation region.

Zachary grew up on "the dark and bloody grounds" of the Kentucky frontier. There were no schools, but the boy studied for a while under tutors, and gained much practical knowledge by working on his father's farm.

The home has been destroyed.

Location:

On Hwy. 33 West between Gordonsville, Virginia and Barboursville, Virginia.

ZACHARY TAYLOR'S HOME
"SPRINGFIELD, LOUISVILLE, KENTUCKY

Zachary Taylor lived at "Springfield" until 1808 when he received a commission as first lieutenant in the 7th U.S. Infantry. In 1810 while on leave, he was married in the home, which was also probably the birthplace of several of his children.

Following Zachary Taylor's death in the White House in 1850, his body was brought back to "Springfield" and entered into the family burial grounds, which later became the nucleus of Zachary Taylor National Cemetery. The home is privately owned.

Location:

5608 Apache Road. 7 miles east on Hwy. 42, Louisville, Kentucky.

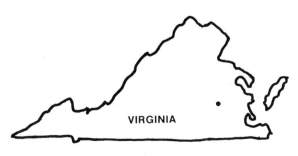

VIRGINIA

• **ZACHARY TAYLOR'S BIRTHPLACE**
"MONTEBELLO" (near) BARBOURSVILLE, VIRGINIA

**ZACHARY TAYLOR'S BURIAL SITE
ZACHARY TAYLOR NATIONAL CEMETERY
LOUISVILLE, KENTUCKY**

On May 6, 1926, the remains of Zachary Taylor and his wife were transferred from an old vault in the Taylor family burying grounds to a new mausoleum erected by the United States Government pursuant to legislation approved February 24, 1925. The mausoleum, of classic Roman design, is constructed of limestone with the exterior lined with marble. Over double glass paneled bronze doors appears the inscription "1784 Zachary Taylor 1850". The Zachary Taylor original family vault may still be seen in the family burial grounds.

Location:

4701 Brownsboro Road. Seven miles east of Louisville, Kentucky, on U.S. Highway 42.

**ORIGINAL FAMILY VAULT MAY STILL BE SEEN
IN THE FAMILY BURIAL GROUNDS**

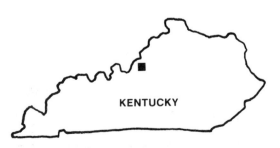

**■ ZACHARY TAYLOR BURIAL SITE
ZACHARY TAYLOR NATIONAL CEMETERY
LOUISVILLE, KENTUCKY**

MILLARD FILLMORE
13th President

**Term - July 9, 1850
to March 4, 1853**

Whig Party

Millard Fillmore

Birth: Locke, Cayuga County, New York. January 7, 1800.
Zodiac Sign: Capricorn.
Ancestry: English
Father: Nathaniel Fillmore. Born: Bennington, Vermont, April 19, 1771. Died: March 28, 1863.
Mother: Phoebe Millard Fillmore. Born: Pittsfield, Massachusetts, 1780. Died: May 2, 1831.
Brothers: Cyrus (1801 - ?). Almon Hopkins (1806 - 1830). Calvin Turner (1810 - ?). Darius Ingraham (1814 - 1837). Charles De Witt (1817 - 1854).
Sisters: Olive Armstrong (1797 - ?). Julia (1812 - ?). Phoebe Maria (1819 - 1843).
First Wife: Abigail Powers. Born: Stillwater, New York, March 13, 1798. Died: Washington, D.C., March 30, 1853. Buried: Forest Lawn Cemetery, Buffalo, New York.
First Marriage: Moravia, New York. February 5, 1826.
Second Wife: Caroline Carmichael McIntosh. Born: Morristown, New Jersey, October 21, 1813. Died: Buffalo, New York, August 11, 1881. Buried: Forest Lawn Cemetery, Buffalo, New York.
Second Marraige: Albany, New York. February 10, 1858.
Children: (by first wife) Millard Powers (1828 - 1889). Mary Abigail (1832 - 1854).
Education: Attended public schools; studied law in Cayuga County and Buffalo, New York.
Religion: Unitarian
Occupation Before Presidency: Lawyer
Pre-Presidential Offices: Member of New York Legislature; Member of U.S. House of Representatives; Vice President of the U.S.
Political Party: Whig, during Presidency; American from 1854.
Age at Inauguration: 50

Note: The second Vice President who succeeded to the Presidency because of the death of his predecessor, Zachary Taylor.
The Fillmore Administration
President: Millard Fillmore
Inauguration: July 10, 1850
Hall of the House of Representatives, Washington, D.C.
President at Time of Death: Ulysses S. Grant
Death: Buffalo, New York. March 8, 1874.
Cause of Death: Debility at age 74.
Place of Burial: Forest Lawn Cemetery, Buffalo, New York

"I think no event would be hailed with more gratification by the people of the United States than the amicable adjustment of questions of difficulty which have now for a long time agitated the country."
— Message to Congress, 1850

MILLARD FILLMORE'S BIRTHPLACE
FILLMORE GLEN STATE PARK
MORAVIA, NEW YORK

Fillmore Glen State Park was named for former President Millard Fillmore who was born at Locke "Summerhill", New York about five miles from the park in a log cabin on January 7, 1800. His parents, Nathaniel and Phoebe Millard Fillmore, had moved to the frontier from Bennington, Vermont.

Millard attended school for only short periods, but he learned reading, spelling, arithmetic and geography. His father owned two books, the Bible, and a hymnbook.

He is remembered for his moral convictions and his concrete actions against the institution of human slavery. A reconstructed cabin, similar to the original, was built at the park as a tribute to a brilliant statesman.

Location:
Hwy. 38, one mile south of Moravia, New York.

MILLARD FILLMORE'S HOME
EAST AURORA, NEW YORK

In 1826, young lawyer, politician and bridegroom, Millard Fillmore, while continuing his odyssey from log cabin to the White House, built the front part of this simple frame residence where his only son was to be born, and lived in it for 4 years before moving to his home, "Gothick Manse" (now the Statler Hilton Hotel), Niagara Square, Buffalo, New York.

In 1930, the present owners moved the structure about a mile to its present location.

A private residence, not open to the public.

Location:
24 Shearer Ave., East Aurora, New York.

• MILLARD FILLMORE'S BIRTHPLACE
FILLMORE GLEN STATE PARK
MORAVIA, NEW YORK

NEW YORK

44

MILLARD FILLMORE'S BURIAL SITE
FOREST LAWN CEMETERY
BUFFALO, NEW YORK

On a gentle slope in Buffalo's Forest Lawn, overlooking Delaware Avenue and Park Lake, stand giant shade trees — silent sentinels surrounding and helping to keep ever sacred the burial place of Millard Fillmore, outstanding Buffalonian, who became the thirteenth President of the United States of America.

Death came to Millard Fillmore on March 8, 1874 — his 74th year. He was buried in his family plot, and as a memorial to him and to his family, there points skyward a dignified obelisk of pink granite. At his own grave there stands a simple granite memorial marker with only two letters, "M F"

A bronze plaque appears on the protective lot enclosure reading:

In Memory
of
Millard Fillmore
13th President of the
United States of America
Born January 7, 1800   Died March 8 1874
Dedicated by the Millard Fillmore Republican Womans Club
Memorial Day, May 30, 1932

Location:
1411 Delaware at Delavan, Buffalo, New York.

NEW YORK

■ **MILLARD FILLMORE'S BURIAL SITE**
FOREST LAWN CEMETERY
BUFFALO, NEW YORK

FRANKLIN PIERCE
14th President

**Term - March 4, 1853
to March 4, 1857**

Democratic Party

Birth: Hillsboro, New Hampshire. November 23, 1804.
Zodiac Sign: Sagittarius
Ancestry: English
Father: Benjamin Pierce. Born: Chelmsford, Massachusetts, December 25, 1757. Died: Hillsboro, New Hampshire, April 1, 1839.
Mother: Anna Kendrick Pierce. Born: Amhert, New Hampshire, 1768. Died: Hillsboro, New Hampshire, December, 1838.
Brothers: Benjamin Kendrick (1790 - 1850). John Sullivan (1796 - 1824). Charles Grandison (1803 - 1828). Henry Dearborn (1812 - 1880).
Sisters: Nancy M. (1792 - 1837). Harriet B. (1800 - 1837).
Half Sister: Elizabeth Andrews (1788 - 1855).
Wife: Jane Means Appleton. Born: Hampton, New Hampshire, March 12, 1806. Died: Andover, Massachusetts, December 2, 1863. Buried: Old North Cemetery, Concord, New Hampshire.
Marriage: Amherst, New Hampshire. November 19, 1834.
Children: Franklin (1836 - 1836). Frank Robert (1839 - 1843). Benjamin (1841 - 1853).
Home: Pierce Homestead, Hillsboro Upper Village, New Hampshire.
Education: Attended public school and Hancock Academy; graduated from Bowdoin College (1824).
Religion: Episcopalian
Occupation Before Presidency: Lawyer, politician, soldier.
Military Service: Brigadier general in U.S. Army (1847 - 1848).
Pre-Presidential Offices: Member and Speaker of New Hampshire Legislature; Member of U.S. House of Representatives; Member of U.S. Senate; President of New Hampshire Constitutional Convention.

Political Party: Democratic
Age at Inauguration: 48
Election of 1852

Candidates	Electoral Vote
Franklin Pierce (Democratic)	254
Winfield Scott (Whig)	42
John P. Hale (Free - Soil)	—

The Pierce Administration
President: Franklin Pierce
Vice President: William R. King of Alabama (died April 18, 1853)
Inauguration: March 4, 1853
The Capitol, Washington, D.C.
Occupation After Presidency: Retired
President at Time of Death: Ulysses S. Grant
Death: Concord, New Hampshire. October 8, 1869.
Cause of Death: Stomach inflammation at age 64.
Place of Burial: Old North Cemetery, Concord, New Hampshire.

"In expressing briefly my view upon an important subject which has recently agitated the nation . . ., I fervently hope that the question is at rest and that no sectional or ambitious or fanatical excitement may again threaten the durability of our institutions."

— Inaugural Address, 1853

**FRANKLIN PIERCE'S BIRTHPLACE
HILLSBORO, NEW HAMPSHIRE**

Franklin Pierce was born in Hillsboro, New Hampshire. The house in which he was born fell into ruin, and nothing remains of it today. The Pierce family moved to this handsome clapboard home in Hillsboro, New Hampshire when Franklin was only three weeks old. He lived here through his early schooling, after his graduation from Bowdoin College and during his early career as a representative from Hillsboro to the the General Court, and later Congressman from New Hampshire.

The mansion, an example of a home of affluence at the beginning of the 19th century, has a ballroom occupying the entire length of the second floor. One front parlor has expensive, stenciled wallpaper imported from Italy.

Location:

3 miles west of Hillsboro, New Hampshire, near Jct. 9 and 31.

**FRANKLIN PIERCE'S BIRTHPLACE
HILLSBORO, NEW HAMPSHIRE**

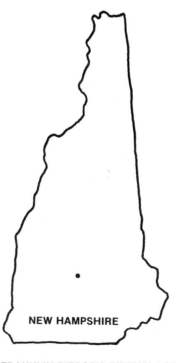

**• FRANKLIN PIERCE'S BIRTHPLACE
HILLSBORO, NEW HAMPSHIRE**

**FRANKLIN PIERCE'S HOME
"PIERCE MANSE," CONCORD, NEW HAMPSHIRE**

Home of President Franklin Pierce from 1842 - 1848. Reconstructed and moved to present site; contains many original furnishings and period pieces.
Location:
    14 Penacook Street, Concord, New Hampshire.

**FRANKLIN PIERCE'S HOUSE
CONCORD, NEW HAMPSHIRE**

The Franklin Pierce house in Concord, New Hampshire, built by a friend while Pierce was President. In 1857, at the expiration of his term, Pierce and his wife, Jane, moved in here, where they lived for the rest of their lives.

Franklin Pierce died in the bedroom, October 8, 1869.
Location:
    52 South Main Street, Concord, New Hampshire.
    Not open.

FRANKLIN PIERCE'S BURIAL SITE
OLD NORTH CEMETERY
CONCORD, NEW HAMPSHIRE

Franklin Pierce lies buried in nearby Minot enclosure. Native son of New Hampshire, graduate of Bowdoin College, lawyer, effective political leader, Congressman and U.S. Senator, Mexican War veteran, courageous advocate of States' Rights, he was popularly known as "Young Hickory of the Granite Hills".

Location:

North State Street, near State Capitol, Concord, New Hampshire.

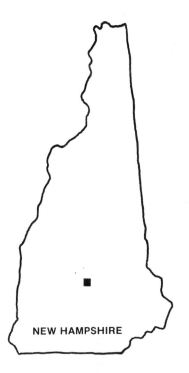

NEW HAMPSHIRE

■ **FRANKLIN PIERCE'S BURIAL SITE**
OLD NORTH CEMETERY
CONCORD, NEW HAMPSHIRE

JAMES BUCHANAN
15th President

Term - March 4, 1857
To March 4, 1861

Democratic Party

Birth: Cove Gap, near Mercersburg, Pennsylvania. April 23, 1791.

Zodiac Sign: Taurus.

Ancestry: Scotch - Irish

Father: James Buchanan. Born: County Donegal, Ireland, 1761. Died: Mercersburg, Pennsylvania, June 11, 1821.

Mother: Elizabeth Speer Buchanan. Born: Lancaster County, Pennsylvania, 1767. Died: Greensburg, Pennsylvania, May 14, 1833.

Brothers: William Speer (1805 - 1826). George Washington (1808 - 1832). Edward Young (1811 - 1895).

Sisters: Mary (1789 - 1791). Jane (1793 - 1839). Maria (1795 - 1849). Sarah (1798 - 1825). Elizabeth (1800 - 1801). Harriet (1802 - 1839).

Home: Wheatland, Lancaster, Pennsylvania

Education: Attended Old Stone Academy; graduated from Dickinson College in 1809.

Religion: Presbyterian

Occupation Before Presidency: Lawyer

Pre-Presidential Offices: Member of Pennsylvania Legislature; Member of U.S. House of Representatives; Minister to Russia; Member of U.S. Senate; Secretary of State; Minister to Great Britain.

Age at Inauguration: 65

Election of 1856

Candidates	Electoral Vote
James Buchanan (Democratic)	174
John Fremont (Republican)	114
Millard Fillmore (American) (Know - Nothing)	8

The Buchanan Administration

President: James Buchanan
Vice President: John C. Breckenridge of Kentucky
Inauguration: March 4, 1857
The Capitol, Washington, D.C.

Occupation After Presidency: Retired

President at Time of Death: Ulysses S. Grant

Death: Lancaster Pennsylvania. June 1, 1868.

Cause of Death: Rheumatic gout at age 77.

Place of Burial: Woodward Hill Cemetery, Lancaster, Pennsylvania.

"Our Union rests upon public opinion, and can never be cemented by the blood of its citizens shed in civil war."
— Message to Congress, 1860

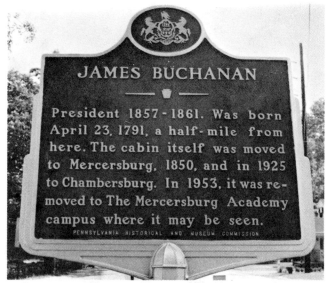

**JAMES BUCHANAN'S BIRTHPLACE
BUCHANAN STATE PARK
STONEY BATTER, PENNSYLVANIA**

**JAMES BUCHANAN'S BIRTHPLACE
MERCERSBURG ACADEMY
MERCERSBURG, PENNSYLVANIA**

This cabin in which James Buchanan was born now stands on the campus of the Mercersburg Academy, Mercersburg, Pennsylvania.

A large plaque has been erected near the cabin listing some of the important events from the life of President Buchanan.

    1820 — Elected to the U.S. House of Representatives
    1831 — Appointed Minister to Russia
    1834 — Elected to the U.S. Senate
    1845 — Appointed Secretary of State
    1853 — Appointed Minister to Great Britain
    1856 — Elected President of the United States

Location:

    On Mercersburg Academy campus, Mercersburg, Pennsylvania.

**JAMES BUCHANAN'S BIRTHPLACE
BUCHANAN STATE PARK
STONEY BATTER, PENNSYLVANIA**

James Buchanan, who became the 15th President of the United States, was born in a log cabin on April 23, 1791, at Stoney Batter, a few miles northwest of Mercersburg, Pennsylvania.

A pyramid of mountain stone marks the original place where the cabin once stood. It is located in Buchanan State Park, near a sparkling mountain stream and surrounded by towering pines, the site is a favorite picnic area.

Location:

    4 miles north of Mercersburg, Pennsylvania on Route 16.

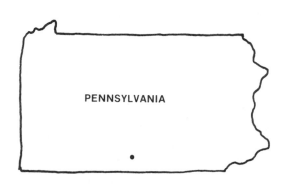

**• JAMES BUCHANAN'S BIRTHPLACE
MERCERSBURG ACADEMY
MERCERSBURG, PENNSYLVANIA**

51

JAMES BUCHANAN'S HOUSE
MERCERSBURG, PENNSYLVANIA

HARRIET LANE HOUSE
JAMES BUCHANAN'S NIECE
MERCERSBURG, PENNSYLVANIA

JAMES BUCHANAN'S HOUSE
MERCERSBURG, PENNSYLVANIA

HARRIET LANE HOUSE
JAMES BUCHANAN'S NIECE
MERCERSBURG, PENNSYLVANIA

Boyhood home of James Buchanan, lawyer, statesman, diplomat, fifteenth President of the United States. Buchanan family moved from Stony Batter to Mercersburg in 1796. From here, James entered Dickinson College in 1807.

Part of this present hotel on Main Street bears James Buchanan's name.

Location:

Main Street, Mercersburg, Pennsylvania.

This home was built by Thomas Lane. It was later occupied by the family of Elliott Lane. Here, Harriet Lane, niece of James Buchanan, and mistress of the White House during his Presidency, was born.

Location:

On Main Street. Across the street from the James Buchanan House, Mercersburg, Pennsylvania.

JAMES BUCHANAN'S BURIAL SITE
WOODWORD HILL CEMETERY
LANCASTER, PENNSYLVANIA

Buchanan retired to "Wheatland" after Lincoln's inauguration and followed the events of the Civil War. He spent much time writing a book in defense of his policies, "Mr. Buchanan's Administration on the Eve of the Rebellion". Harriet Lane and a nephew, James Buchanan Henry, lived with him during his last years.

Buchanan died on June 1, 1868. He was buried in Woodward Hill Cemetery in Lancaster, Pennsylvania.
Location:

538 East Strawberry Street, Lancaster, Pennsylvania.

JAMES BUCHANAN'S HOME
"WHEATLAND," LANCASTER, PENNSYLVANIA

"Wheatland", the home of President James Buchanan, is designated by the United States Department of the Interior as a Registered Historic Landmark.

In the troubled years before the Civil War, it was one of the most famous country homes in the nation. Statesmen from all parts of the nation came here in the 1850's to meet James Buchanan and his lovely niece, Harriet Lane, on the front porch and to be entertained graciously in the quiet rooms or on the brood lawn.

"Wheatland" is a symbol of the comfortable country living which was so characteristic of American life a century ago, before the rise of the city and the age of industry.

The mansion was built in 1828 by a Lancaster banker, who named it "The Wheatlands" because it was located with a view of waving grainfields.

In 1848, James Buchanan, Secretary of State in Polk's cabinet, purchased the home for $6,750 from William Meredith, its second owner.

Buchanan was the nation's only bachelor President, and his lovely niece, Miss Harriet Lane acted as hostess at "Wheatland" and later as First Lady in the White House.
Location:

1120 Marietta Avenue, Lancaster, Pennsylvania.

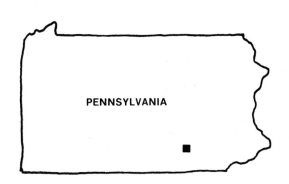

■ JAMES BUCHANAN'S BURIAL SITE
WOODWARD HILL CEMETERY
LANCASTER, PENNSYLVANIA

ABRAHAM LINCOLN
16th President

**Term - March 4, 1861
to April 15, 1865**

Republican Party

Abraham Lincoln

Birth: Sinking Spring Farm, Hardin County, Kentucky. February 12, 1809.

Zodiac Sign: Aquarius.

Ancestry: English

Father: Thomas Lincoln. Born: Rockingham County, Virginia, January 6, 1778. Died: Coles County, Illinois, January 15, 1851.

Mother: Nancy Hanks Lincoln. Born: Cambell County, Virginia, February 5, 1784. Died: Spencer County, Indiana, October 5, 1818.

Stepmother: Sarah Bush Johnston. Born: Hardin County, Kentucky, December 12, 1788. Died: Charleston, Illinois, April 10, 1869.

Brother: Thomas (? - 1812).

Sister: Sarah (1807 - 1828).

Wife: Mary Todd. Born: Lexington, Kentucky, December 13, 1818. Died: Springfield, Illinois, July 16, 1882. Buried: Oak Ridge Cemetery, Springfield, Illinois.

Marriage: Springfield, Illinois, November 4, 1842.

Children: Robert Todd (1843 - 1926). Edward Baker (1846 - 1850). William Wallace (1850 - 1862). Thomas ("Tad") (1852 - 1871).

Home: Eighth and Jackson Streets. Springfield, Illinois.

Education: Local tutors, self-educated.

Religion: No specific denomination.

Occupation Before Presidency: Store clerk; store owner; ferry pilot; surveyor; postmaster; lawyer.

Military Service: Served in volunteer company for three months during Black Hawk War (1832).

Pre-Presidential Offices: Member Illinois General Assembly; Member U.S. House of Representatives.

Age at Inauguration: 52

Election of 1860

Candidates	Electoral Vote
Abraham Lincoln (Republican)	180
Stephen Douglas (Democratic)	12
John C. Breckenridge (Southern Democratic)	72
John Bell (Constitutional Union)	39

First Administration
President: Abraham Lincoln
Vice President: Hannibal Hamlin of Maine
Inauguration: March 4, 1861
The Capitol, Washington, D.C.

Election of 1864
(Because eleven Southern states had seceded from the Union and did not participate in the Presidential election, eighty-one electoral votes were not cast.)

Candidates	Electoral Vote
Abraham Lincoln (National Union)	212
George McClellan (Democratic)	21

Second Administration
President: Abraham Lincoln
Vice President: Andrew Johnson of Tennessee
Inauguration: March 4, 1865
The Capitol, Washington, D.C.

Death: Washington, D.C. April 15, 1865.

Cause of Death: Assassination at age 56. Shot by John Wilkes Booth, April 14, 1865, Ford's Theatre, Washington, D.C.

Place of Burial: Oak Ridge Cemetery, Springfield, Illinois.

"Why should there not be a patient confidence in the ultimate justice of the people? Is there any better or equal hope in the world?"

— Inaugural Address, 1861

**ABRAHAM LINCOLN'S BIRTHPLACE
LINCOLN MEMORIAL BUILDING
HODGENVILLE, KENTUCKY**

A cool limestone spring, called the Sinking Spring, flows here today as it did on February 12, 1809, when Abraham Lincoln was born within the sound of its water.

Memorial Building (1911)

More than 100,000 persons contributed funds to construct this granite and marble building. Inside is the log cabin traditionally believed to be the Lincoln birthplace. The cabin was here on Sinking Spring Farm in 1860; it was disassembled, moved, exhibited and stored many timed before being permanently reconstructed inside the Memorial Building.

Location:

3 miles south of Hodgenville, Kentucky on U.S. 31E and Ky. 61.

**LINCOLN HOMESTEAD
STATE PARK, SPRINGFIELD, KENTUCKY**

In a compound framed by split rail fences is a replica of the cabin built on this land which was originally settled in 1782 by Abraham Lincoln, Sr., grandfather of the President. This was the home of Abraham Lincoln's father, Thomas Lincoln, until he was 25. Furnished in pioneer style, including several pieces made by Thomas Lincoln. Also the Berry House, home of Nancy Hanks during her courtship by Thomas Lincoln: pioneer relics, photostatic copies of the Thomas and Nancy Lincoln marriage bonds.

Location:

5 miles north of Springfield, Kentucky on Ky. 528.

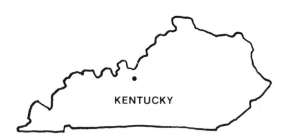

**• ABRAHAM LINCOLN'S BIRTHPLACE
LINCOLN MEMORIAL BUILDING
HODGENVILLE, KENTUCKY**

55

**LINCOLN MARRIAGE TEMPLE
OLD FORT HARROD STATE PARK
HARRODSBURG, KENTUCKY**

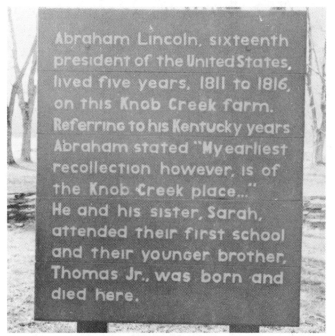

**LINCOLN FARM
"KNOB CREEK", HODGENVILLE, KENTUCKY**

This brick building shelters the cabin where Abraham Lincoln's parents were married. The cabin was removed from the original site near Springfield, Kentucky, where Thomas Lincoln and Nancy Hanks were married June 12, 1806.
Location:
On U.S. 68/127 in Harrodsburg, Kentucky.

**LINCOLN FARM
"KNOB CREEK", HODGENVILLE, KENTUCKY**

**LINCOLN FARM
"KNOB CREEK", HODGENVILLE, KENTUCKY**

Abraham Lincoln, sixteenth president of the United States, lived five years, 1811 to 1816, on this Knob Creek farm. Referring to his Kentucky years Abraham stated "My earliest recollection however, is of the Knob Creek place..." He and his sister, Sarah, attended their first school and their younger brother, Thomas Jr., was born and died here.

Reconstructed cabin where Abraham lived from age two to seven.
Location:
Northeast of Hodgenville, Kentucky on Hwy. 31E.

56

LINCOLN HOMESITE

Cast in bronze, the hearth and sill logs of a pioneer cabin symbolize the traditional site of a log cabin home built by Thomas Lincoln and his son, Abraham. Here the Lincolns cleared, fenced and worked 20 acres of good crop land. Here Abraham Lincoln grew up.

**LINCOLN BOYHOOD HOME
NATIONAL MEMORIAL
LINCOLN CITY, INDIANA**

**NANCY HANKS LINCOLN BURIAL SITE
LINCOLN BOYHOOD HOME
LINCOLN CITY, INDIANA**

Here is the grave of Nancy Hanks Lincoln, mother of Abraham Lincoln. She was 35 years old, and young Abraham was 9 years old when she died October 5, 1818. Thomas Lincoln hammered together a rough wooden coffin and the family buried wife and mother on a wooden knoll south of the cabin.

Location:
South of Lincoln City, Indiana on Ind. 162.

**LINCOLN BOYHOOD HOME
NATIONAL MEMORIAL
LINCOLN CITY, INDIANA**

Abraham Lincoln spent 14 years of his boyhood in this vicinity, reading books, working as a clerk for a nearby merchant and helping his father with his farm work.

Location:
South of Lincoln City, Indiana on Ind. 162.

NANCY HANKS LINCOLN BURIAL GROUNDS

This wooded knoll served as a community cemetery until the end of the Nineteenth Century. Many friends and neighbors of the Lincoln family are buried here. Several of them, like Nancy Hanks Lincoln, died of the dreaded "Milk Sickness".

THE RUTLEDGE TAVERN
LINCOLN'S NEW SALEM STATE PARK
NEW SALEM, ILLINOIS

James Rutledge built the Rutledge Tavern in New Salem probably in the fall of 1828. As originally erected, it contained two large log rooms with loft above. The two frame rooms on the south were added later either by Rutledge or another proprietor of the tavern. When Lincoln boarded at the tavern he slept in the loft.
Location:
2 miles south of Petersburg, Illinois on Ill. 97 and 123.

New Salem, Illinois.

Complete restoration of New Salem as it was when Lincoln lived there.

ANN RUTLEDGE'S BURIAL SITE
OAKLAND CEMETERY, PETERSBURG, ILLINOIS

Ann Rutledge, Lincoln's first sweetheart died in 1835, the daughter of a tavern keeper. Everyone had liked this unaffected girl with her pretty blue eyes and auburn hair. Abe, who once had boarded at her father's tavern was devoted to the Rutledges and doubtless to their daughter as well.

When at 21 Ann died from a baffling illness (probably typhoid fever), Abe, like many residents of New Salem was deeply affected.
Location:
Oakland Cemetery, Oakland Avenue, Petersburg, Illinois.

**MARY TOOD LINCOLN'S HOUSE
LEXINGTON, KENTUCKY**

Girlhood home of Mary Todd, wife of President Abraham Lincoln, is authentically restored. Period furnishings, personal items.

Location:

578 West Main Street, Lexington, Kentucky.

**NINIAN W. EDWARD'S MANSION
ABRAHAM LINCOLN AND MARY TODD'S MARRIAGE SITE
SPRINGFIELD, ILLINOIS**

On the morning of November 4, 1842, Lincoln announced to his future brother-in-law, Ninian W. Edwards that he planned to marry Mary Todd that very day. This surprising news threw the Edward's household into a frenzy of preparation. That evening by candle light, Lincoln and Mary exchanged vows. "Nothing new here", Lincoln wrote a fellow lawyer soon afterwards, "except my marrying, which, to me, is a matter of profound wonder".

Location:

406 South 8th Street, Springfield, Illinois.

**ABRAHAM LINCOLN'S HOME
SPRINGFIELD, ILLINOIS**

The Lincoln Home National Historic Site is the only home Abraham Lincoln ever owned. It was purchased by Lincoln in May 1844, and the Lincoln family lived in the residence until they departed for Washington in 1861. Three of four sons, Edward, William, and Thomas were born in the house. The Lincoln's second son, Edward died in this house after an illness of almost two months.

Location:
    526 South 7th Street at Jackson Street, Springfield, Illinois.

**FORD'S THEATRE
LINCOLN ASSASSINATED
WASHINGTON, D.C.**

On the evening of April 14, 1865, Abraham Lincoln attended a performance of "Our American Cousin" at Ford's Theatre in Washington, D.C. A few minutes after 10 o'clock, a shot rang through the crowded house. John Wilkes Booth, one of the best known actors of the day, had shot the President in the head from the rear of the Presidential box. In leaping to the stage, Booth caught his spur in a flag draped in front of the box. He fell and broke his leg. But he limped across the stage brandishing a dagger and crying: "Sic semper tyrannis" (Thus ever to tyrants), the motto of Virginia.

In basement is Lincoln Museum with exhibits depicting several periods in Lincoln's life.

Location:
    511 - 10th Street N.W., Washington, D.C.

PETERSEN HOME
HOUSE WHERE LINCOLN DIED
WASHINGTON, D.C.

Lincoln was carried from Ford's Theatre, unconscious to the Petersen House. His family and high government officials surrounded him. He died at 7:22 AM on April 15, 1865.

Location:

516 - 10th Street N.W., Washington, D.C.

Abraham Lincoln was buried in Oak Ridge Cemetery at the request of Mrs. Lincoln.

On the day of the funeral, May 4, 1865, Lincoln's body was placed in a receiving vault at the foot of the hill north of the tomb. This vault may still be seen. The body remained there until December of that year when it was moved to a temporary vault on the hillside northeast of the present tomb. It was transferred in 1871 to a crypt in the partially completed monument, and the temporary tomb was removed.

On the cenotaph itself is the simple inscription "Abraham Lincoln, 1809 - 1865". Surrounding it are four flags of the states in which generations of the Lincoln family lived — Massachusetts, New Jersey, Pennsylvania, Virginia and the three flags of Kentucky, Indiana, and Illinois where Lincoln lived, with the national colors and the presidential flag. Inscribed over the window at the north are the words, "Now he belongs to the ages", which were spoken by Secretary of War, Edwin M. Stanton, at Lincoln's death.

Location:

End of Monument Ave., Springfield, Illinois.

ABRAHAM LINCOLN'S BURIAL SITE
OAK RIDGE CEMETERY
SPRINGFIELD, ILLINOIS

■ **ABRAHAM LINCOLN'S BURIAL SITE**
OAK RIDGE CEMETERY
SPRINGFIELD, ILLINOIS

JEFFERSON DAVIS
CONFEDERATE PRESIDENT

**Term - February 18, 1861
to April 9, 1865**

Jefferson Davis

Birth: Fairview, Kentucky. June 3, 1808.

Zodiac Sign: Gemini.

Ancestry: Welsh - Scotch - Irish

Father: Samuel Davis. Born: 1756. Died: 1824.

Mother: Jane Simpson Cook. Born: 1760/61. Died: 1845.

Brothers: Joseph Emory (1784 - 1870). Benjamin (1787/88 - 1827). Samuel (1788/89 - 1835). Isaac Williams (1792 - 1860).

Sisters: Anna Eliza (1791 - 1870). Lucinda Farrar (1797 - 1873). Amanda Jane (1800 - 1881). Matilda (1801 - died as an infant). Mary Ellen (1806 - 1824).

First Wife: Sarah Knox Taylor. Born: Fort Knox, Vincennes, Indiana, March 6, 1814. Died: West Feliciana Parish, Louisiana, September 15, 1835. Buried: Locust Grove Cemetery near St. Francisville, Louisiana.

Marriage: Near Louisville, Kentucky. June 17, 1835.

Second Wife: Varina Anne Banks Howell. Born: 1826. Died: New York City, New York, 1906.

Marriage: "The Briars", near Natchez, Mississippi. February 26, 1845.

Children: Samuel Emory (1852 - 1854). Margaret Howell (1855 - 1909). Jefferson Finis, Jr. (1857 - 1878). Joseph Evan (1859 - 1864). William Howell (1861 - 1872). Varina Anne (1864 - 1898).

Education: St. Thomas College, (a Catholic school), Washington County, Kentucky; Jefferson College, Natchez, Mississippi; Transylvania University, Lexington, Kentucky; United States Military Academy, West Point.

Religion: Episcopalian

Occupation Before Presidency: U.S. House of Representatives; U.S. Senator; Secretary of War under President Franklin Pierce.

Military Service: Lieutenant U.S. Army; Colonel U.S. Army.

Death: New Orleans, Louisiana, December 6, 1889.

Buried: Metairie Cemetery, New Orleans, Louisiana. May 31, 1893. Reinterred in Hollywood Cemetery, Richmond, Virginia.

(Author's note) It seems to me that this book would be incomplete without a page in honor of the gentleman, Jefferson Davis, who served as a leader of over nine million (1/3 were Negro slaves) inhabitants of our Nation at a difficult time in the course of American history.

JEFFERSON DAVIS' BIRTHPLACE
FAIRVIEW, KENTUCKY

JEFFERSON DAVIS' BOYHOOD HOME
"ROSEMONT", WOODVILLE, MISSISSIPPI

This monument, a cast-concrete obelisk, ranks as the fourth tallest in the country at 351 feet, and the tallest of such material. It marks the birthplace of Jefferson Davis, the only President of the Confederate States of America. Overlooking a 20 acre park, the monument was built at a cost of $200,000 raised by public subscription and was dedicated in 1924. Visitors may take an elevator to the top to view the area.

The son of a Revolutionary War officer, Jefferson Davis was born here in 1808, less than 100 miles from Abraham Lincoln's birthplace.

Location:

11 miles east of Hopkinsville on U.S. 68 in Fairview, Kentucky.

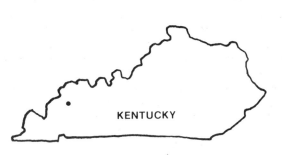

• JEFFERSON DAVIS' BIRTHPLACE
FAIRVIEW, KENTUCKY

DAVIS FAMILY CEMETERY
"ROSEMONT", WOODVILLE, MISSISSIPPI

**JEFFERSON DAVIS' BOYHOOD HOME
"ROSEMONT", WOODVILLE, MISSISSIPPI**

Samuel Davis, Jefferson Davis' father built Rosemont in 1810.

The youngest of ten children, Jefferson Davis was two years old when the family moved here from Kentucky.

Many Davis furnishings remain in the home, among them a spinning wheel that Jane Davis brought with her to Rosemont.

Five generations of the Davis family are buried in the cemetery at Rosemont. Jane Cooke Davis, Jefferson Davis' mother, died in 1845 and is buried in the family cemetery.

Location:

1 mile east of Woodville, Mississippi on the left side of State Hwy. 24, Woodville, Mississippi.

**SARAH KNOX DAVIS' BURIAL SITE
FIRST WIFE OF JEFFERSON DAVIS
(near) ST. FRANCISVILLE, LOUISIANA**

Lieutenant Jefferson Davis fell in love with Sarah, daughter of his commanding officer, Colonel Zachary Taylor, later President of the United States. Despite Colonel Taylor's strong opposition, the young couple got married. Davis resigned from the army in 1835, taking his charming bride to his plantation, "Briefield". It was located 15 miles south of Vicksburg, Mississippi.

As the summer fever season came on, Jefferson decided to take his bride to a more healthy place for a time. They went to visit his sister at Bayou Sara, Louisiana. Shortly thereafter Jefferson became ill with malarial fever, and the next day Knox came down with the same. They were put in separate rooms and Jefferson, being too ill at the time, was not told of her condition. Her delirious condition precluded any anxiety on her part with respect to Jefferson. Knox's fever rose so high that shortly she succumbed to it. Hearing her singing loudly a song called "Fairy Bells", Jefferson, as sick as he was, staggered to her bedside to see her take her last breath. The tragic and untimely death on September 17, 1835, took his bride of barely three months and just seven months past her twenty-first birthday. The grief-stricken young planter remained in seclusion for some years, but gradually he became active in politics. In 1845 he was elected to Congress. That same year he married Varina Howell, a brilliant young girl of Natchez, Mississippi.

Location:

Locust Grove Cemetery, Near St. Francisville, Louisiana.

Civil War
1861 - 1865

Confederate States of America was the name taken by six southern states when they organized their government at Montgomery, Alabama, in February, 1861. The states seceded (withdrew) ·from the government of the United States in 1860 and 1861 because they feared that the election of Abraham Lincoln, a Republican President, might lead to restrictions on their right to do as they chose about the question of Negro slavery. The first state to leave the Union was South Carolina on December 20, 1860. Mississippi, Florida, Alabama, Georgia, and Louisiana followed South Carolina's lead in January, 1861. On February 1, 1861, Texas, North Carolina, and Tennessee joined the ranks to make eleven confederate states in all.

Organization of a government for the Confederacy began on February 4, 1861. when delegates from 6 of the 7 seceding states met as Montgomery, Alabama, and set up a temporary government. Jefferson Davis of Mississippi was elected President of the Confederacy and Alexander H. Stephens of Georgia was chosen Vice President.

The Constitution of the Confederacy, adopted in March, 1861, was modeled after the United States Constitution, but it contained six important differences -

1.   The term of the President and Vice President was six years. The President was not allowed to succeed himself.

2.   Members of the cabinet received seats in Congress, with the privilege of debate, but they could not vote.

3.   Foreign slave trade was prohibited, but not slavery.

4.   Congress was forbidden to make appropriations for internal improvements, to levy a protective tariff, or to give bounties.

5.   A two .thirds vote of both houses of Congress was necessary to admit a new state into the Confederacy or to make appropriations not requested by the heads of departments through the President.

6.   The President could veto single items in appropriations bills.

The Confederate States hoped for a peaceful withdrawal from the Union. A number of persons in the Confederacy and in the Union worked hard to avoid war. But their efforts failed, and war began with the attack of Fort Sumter on April 12, 1861.

Location:

Bainbridge between Washington and Monroe Avenues, Montgomery, Alabama.

ALABAMA STATE CAPITOL
FIRST CAPITOL OF THE CONFEDERATE STATES OF AMERICA
MONTGOMERY, ALABAMA

First capitol of the Confederate States of America, in Montgomery, is also the present state capitol.

Alabama withdrew from the Union on January 11, 1861, and declared itself the Republic of Alabama. The Alabama secession convention invited other southern states to send delegates to Montgomery. On February 8, 1861, the convention established the Confederate States of America in the present Senate chamber, with Montgomery as its capital. Montgomery is often called the Cradle of the Confederacy.

A six-pointed brass star at the top of the steps on the west portico marks the spot where Jefferson Davis took his oath of office as President of the Confederate States of America on February 18, 1861.

**FIRST WHITE HOUSE OF THE
CONFEDERATE STATES OF AMERICA
MONTGOMERY, ALABAMA**

**FIRST WHITE HOUSE OF THE
CONFEDERATE STATES OF AMERICA
MONTGOMERY, ALABAMA**

This two-story white frame house built in 1852 was the residence of President Jefferson Davis and his family for only three months. Moved from its original location at Bibb, Moulton, and Lee Streets in 1921, it is now a confederate shrine containing period furnishings, many personal belongings, and paintings of the Davis family and confederate relics of the Montgomery area.

Location;

Washington Ave. and Union Street, Montgomery, Alabama.

**VIRGINIA STATE CAPITOL
SECOND CAPITOL OF THE
CONFEDERATE STATES OF AMERICA
RICHMOND, VIRGINIA**

After Virginia joined the Confederacy, the capital was moved from Montgomery, Alabama to Richmond, Virginia.

The old hall of the house was the scene of many important events. The state secession convention of 1861 met here during the later part of its historic first session.

On April 23, 1861, General Robert E. Lee appeared before the secession convention in the capitol and accepted command of the army forces of Virginia.

On Sunday, April 2, 1865, Jefferson Davis told his cabinet that the government must move immediately to Danville, Virginia.

Location:

9 and Grace Streets, Richmond, Virginia.

66

**SECOND WHITE HOUSE OF THE
CONFEDERATE STATES OF AMERICA
RICHMOND, VIRGINIA**

**DANVILLE MUSEUM OF FINE ARTS AND HISTORY
LAST CAPITOL OF THE CONFEDERATE STATES OF AMERICA
DANVILLE, VIRGINIA**

This historic building served as the official residence of Confederate President Jefferson Davis during the war between the states.

President Davis and his family resided in this house from August 1, 1861, until April 2, 1865. During these years the White House of the Confederacy became the social as well as a political center.

In the spring of 1864, tragedy visited the house when little Joe Davis, the President's five year old son, fell to his death from the porch of the mansion. Less than one year later, on the first Sunday in April, President Davis and the entire Confederate government evacuated Richmond, leaving the city and their White House to the disposition of rapidly advancing Union forces.

Location:

1201 East Clay Street, Richmond, Virginia.

**DANVILLE MUSEUM OF FINE ARTS AND HISTORY
LAST CAPITOL OF THE CONFEDERATE STATES OF AMERICA
DANVILLE, VIRGINIA**

Jefferson Davis and his cabinet met here during the last days of the Confederacy (April 3-10, 1865). Davis held his last full cabinet meeting in this home, of Major W.T. Sutherlin. The establishment of the Confederate Government in Danville ended when the news of Lee's surrender arrived on April 10, 1865.

Location:

975 Main Street, Danville, Virginia.

THE McLEAN HOUSE
APPOMATTOX COURT HOUSE HISTORICAL PARK
APPOMATTOX, VIRGINIA

JEFFERSON DAVIS' CASEMATE
FORT MONROE, VIRGINIA

THE McLEAN HOUSE
APPOMATTOX COURT HOUSE HISTORICAL PARK
APPOMATTOX, VIRGINIA

Here in the parlor of Wilmer McLean's home on April 9, 1865, Palm Sunday, General Robert E. Lee surrendered the army of northern Virginia to General Ulysses Grant. This act brought the Civil War to an end.

Location:

3 miles north east of Appomattox, Virginia on Virginia 24, Appomattox, Virginia.

**JEFFERSON DAVIS' CASEMATE
FORT MONROE, VIRGINIA**

Jefferson Davis, the President of the Confederate States · has become America's most famous political prisoner as the results of his imprisonment in a casemate, which is a chamber in the wall of a fort, at Fort Monroe on Old Point Comfort, Virginia. The cell, with its whitewashed stone walls and barred windows overlooking the green waters of the moat surrounding the fort, recalls vividly that fateful day of May 22, 1865, when Jefferson Davis, falsely accused of plotting the assassination of Abraham Lincoln, entered as a prisoner of the Union Army.

On May 13, 1867, Jefferson Davis was released at Richmond, Virginia Courthouse on a bail bond for $100,000 signed by Horace Greeley, Cornelius Vanderbilt and Augustus Schell.

Location:

From Williamsburg, Virginia, south on Route 168, Interstate 64 to Exit 5, left on 143 to Fort Monroe, Virginia.

**JEFFERSON DAVIS' SHRINE
"BEAUVOIR", MIDWAY BETWEEN BILOXI
AND GULFPORT, MISSISSIPPI**

This is the home in which Confederate President Jefferson Davis spent the last 12 years of his life. Here he wrote his two volume work "The Rise and Fall of the Confederate Government". This work he declared to be a defense and not a history: "The other side has written and is writing their statement of the case. We wish to present ours also, that the future historian by considering both may deduce the unbiased statement which no contemporary could make . . . . We want our side of the war and exactly stated, that the men who come after us may compare and do justice in the case."

Location:

5 miles west on West Beach Blvd. (U.S. 90), Biloxi, Mississippi.

**JEFFERSON DAVIS' BURIAL SITE
HOLLYWOOD CEMETERY, RICHMOND, VIRGINIA**

Returning ill from a visit to "Brierfield" in 1889, Jefferson Davis never reached home. When his boat docked in New Orleans, he was too ill to be taken to Beauvoir and he was removed to the home of one of his friends. With his wife at his bedside, Davis lay ill from mid-November until shortly after midnight on the early morning of December 6, 1889, at 12:45 when finally he drew his last breath.

Davis was buried in Metairie Cemetery in New Orleans. Many states wanted to be the permanent burial place for Jefferson Davis. Kentucky wanted him because he was her native son and had spent years in school there and his first marriage had been in Louisville; most of his life had been spent in Mississippi; Alabama claimed him because he had been elected President of the Confederate States in Montgomery; Georgia wanted him because his father was a native of Georgia; Tennessee laid claim to him because he had lived and worked in Memphis after the war; Virginia argued that she was the burial ground of many former presidents and great names that filled the pages of American history. Had not Jefferson Davis been President of the Confederate States with Richmond as the capital? Stating that Richmond was the proper place, Mrs. Davis agreed and gave her consent so Virginia won the claim. In May, 1893, Jefferson Davis was removed from New Orleans and carried by train to his final resting place. On May 31, 1893, Jefferson Davis was with full military honors, reinterred in Hollywood Cemetery in Richmond, Virginia near the James River.

Location:

412 South Cherry Street at Albermarle Street, Richmond, Virginia.

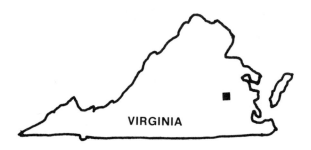

**■ JEFFERSON DAVIS' BURIAL SITE
HOLLYWOOD CEMETERY
RICHMOND, VIRGINIA**

ANDREW JOHNSON
17th President

**Term - April 15, 1865
to March 4, 1869**

Democratic Party

Birth: Raleigh, North Carolina. December 29, 1808.
Zodiac Sign: Capricorn
Ancestry: Scotch - Irish and English
Father: Jacob Johnson. Born: Northumberland County, England, April 5, 1778. Died: Raleigh, North Carolina, January 4, 1812.
Mother: Mary McDonough Johnson. Born: July 17, 1783. Died: February 13, 1856.
Brother: William (1804 - ?).
Wife: Eliza McCardle. Born: Leesburg, Tennessee, October 4, 1810. Died: Greene County, Tennessee, January 15, 1876. Buried: Andrew Johnson National Cemetery, Greeneville, Tennessee.
Marriage: Greeneville, Tennessee. May 5, 1827.
Children: Martha (1828 - 1901). Charles (1830 - 1863). Mary (1832 - 1883). Robert (1834 - 1869). Andrew (1852 - 1879).
Home: Greeneville, Tennessee
Education: Self-taught
Religion: No specific denomination
Occupation Before Presidency: Tailor; legislator.
Pre-Presidential Offices: Alderman; Mayor; Member of Tennessee Legislature; Member of U.S. House of Representatives; Governor of Tennessee; Member of U.S. Senate; Vice President of the U.S.
Political Party; Democratic; elected Vice President on National Union ticket.
Age at Inauguration: 56
Note: The third Vice President who succeeded to the Presidency because of the death of his predecessor, Abraham Lincoln.
The Johnson Administration
President: Andrew Johnson
Inauguration: April 15, 1865
Kirkwood House, Washington, D.C.

Occupation After Presidency: Senator
President at Time of Death: Ulysses S. Grant
Death: Carter County, Tennessee. July 31, 1875.
Cause of Death: Stroke at age 66.
Place of Burial: Andrew Johnson National Cemetery, Greeneville, Tennessee.

"It is our sacred duty to transmit unimpaired to our posterity the blessings of liberty, which were bequeathed to us by the founders of the Republic . . ."
— Message to Congress, 1868

**ANDREW JOHNSON'S BIRTHPLACE
MORDECAI HISTORIC PARK
RALEIGH, NORTH CAROLINA**

Andrew Johnson was born in Raleigh, North Carolina on December 29, 1808. This reconstructed cabin stands in Mordicai Historic Park.

Andrew Johnson's parents were poor and uneducated, and Johnson himself had no formal schooling, learning to read and write at the age of ten. He and his brother were raised in this house by their mother, the father having died when Andrew was three.

Location:

1 Mimosa Street, Raleigh, North Carolina.

**ANDREW JOHNSON'S BIRTHPLACE
MORDECAI HISTORIC PARK
RALEIGH, NORTH CAROLINA**

**• ANDREW JOHNSON'S BIRTHPLACE
MORDECAI HISTORIC PARK
RALEIGH, NORTH CAROLINA**

**ANDREW JOHNSON'S HOMESTEAD
GREENEVILLE, TENNESSEE**

The Johnson Homestead occupied by the Johnson family, 1851 - 1875 during the period in which he attained success in politics. Restored and furnished with many family heirlooms.
Location:
    College and Main Streets, Greeneville, Tennessee.

Nearby is the Visitor Center. A brick building shelters the Johnson tailor shop, restored with some original furnishings and tools of his craft as well as a museum with exhibits and memorabilia relating to Johnson's career.
Location:
    Depot and College Streets, Greeneville, Tennessee.

ANDREW JOHNSON National Cemetery

In fulfillment of his own request, Andrew Johnson's body lies wrapped in the American flag, his head resting on a copy of the Constitution. On his monument the eagle and flag symbolize his loyalty to the Union; the open Bible, his faith in God and man; and the scroll, his esteem for the Constitution of the United States.

The marble shaft was erected by his family in 1878.

**ANDREW JOHNSON NATIONAL CEMETERY
GREENEVILLE, TENNESSEE**

73

ANDREW JOHNSON'S BURIAL SITE
ANDREW JOHNSON NATIONAL CEMETERY
GREENEVILLE, TENNESSEE

On August 3, 1875, a stately funeral procession moved through the streets of Greeneville, its destination the cone-shaped summit of Signal Hill in the western edge of the city to which Andrew Johnson, according to family tradition, was wont to go for relaxation and meditation. Now, as he had requested in life, this site was to be his last resting place. One notable feature of the day was the presence of an exceedingly large number of what were known as the "plain people". The farmers and mechanics, the honest yeomanry were out in force, and showed unmistakably the hold he had upon that class. He had been one of them, traveling over the same path of daily toil that they had tread, and knew how to sympathize with them in their hardships. Their mute and inexpressible grief told how they regarded his death. A bouquet of white lilies and roses, held together by white satin ribbon, bearing the mottoes, "The People's Friend", "He Sleepeth", was laid on the grave.

In fulfillment of his request, Andrew Johnson's body lies wrapped in the American flag, his head resting on a copy of the Constitution. On his monument, the eagle and flag symbolize his loyalty to the Union; the open Bible, his faith in God and man; and the scroll, his esteem for the Constitution of the United States.

Location:
Grave and monument south of Greeneville, Tennessee on Monument Avenue, Greeneville, Tennessee.

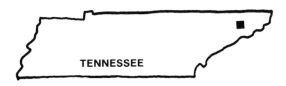

■ ANDREW JOHNSON'S BURIAL SITE
ANDREW JOHNSON NATIONAL CEMETERY
GREENEVILLE, TENNESSEE

ULYSSES S. GRANT
18th President

**Term — March 4, 1869
to March 4, 1877**

Republican Party

Birth: Point Pleasant, Ohio. April 27, 1822.
Zodiac Sign: Taurus.
Ancestry: English - Scotch
Father: Jesse Root Grant. Born: near Greensburg, Westmoreland County, Pennsylvania, January 23, 1794. Died: Covington, Kentucky, June 29, 1873.
Mother: Hannah Simpson Grant. Born: Montgomery County, Pennsylvania, November 23, 1798. Died: Jersey City, New Jersey, May 11, 1883.
Brothers: Samuel Simpson (1825 - 1861). Orvil Lynch (1835 - 1881).
Sisters: Clara Rachel (1828 - 1865). Virginia Paine (1832 - 1881). Mary Frances (1839 - 1898).
Wife: Julia Boggs Dent. Born: St. Louis. Missouri, January 26, 1826. Died: Washington, D.C., December 14, 1902. Buried: Grant's Tomb, New York, New York.
Marriage: St. Louis, Missouri. August 22, 1848.
Children: Frederick Dent (1850 - 1912). Ulysses Simpson (1852 - 1929). Ellen Wrenshall (1855 - 1922). Jesse Root (1858 - 1934).
Education: Local schools, U.S. Military Academy.
Religion: Methodist
Occupation Before Presidency: Soldier; farmer; real-estate agent; custom house clerk; leather store clerk.
Military Service: Commissioned 2nd Lt. in 4th U.S. Infantry (1843), resigned at Captain (1854), re-entered Army in August 1861 as brig. general; became general in chief of Union armies on March 12, 1864.
Age at Inauguration: 46
Election of 1868

Candidates	Electoral Vote
Ulysses S. Grant (Republican)	214
Horatio Seymour (Democratic)	80

First Administration
President: Ulysses S. Grant
Vice President: Schuyler Colfax of Indiana
Inauguration: March 4, 1869
The Capitol, Washington, D.C.
Election of 1872
(Horace Greeley died shortly after the election, and the 66 electoral votes he had won were cast for several Democratic candidates.)

Candidates	Electoral Vote
Ulysses S. Grant (Republican)	286
Horace Greeley (Democratic)	—

Second Administration
President: Ulysses S. Grant
Vice President: Henry Wilson of Massachusetts
Inauguration: March 4, 1873
The Capitol, Washington, D.C.
President at Time of Death: Grover Cleveland
Death: Mount McGregor, New York. July 23, 1885.
Cause of Death: Cancer at age 63.
Place of Burial: Grant's Tomb, New York, New York.

"I ask patient forbearance one toward another throughout the land, and a determined effort on the part of every citizen to do his share toward cementing a happy Union."

— Inaugural Address, 1869

ULYSSES S. GRANT'S BIRTHPLACE
OHIO STATE MEMORIAL, POINT PLEASANT, OHIO

Ulysses S. Grant was born on April 27, 1822, in Point Pleasant, Ohio, a village on the Ohio River about 20 miles south east of Cincinnati. He was the first child of Jesse and Hannah Simpson Grant. They named their son Hiram Ulysses Grant, but always called him Ulysses or 'Lyss. The year after Ulysses was born, the family moved to nearby Georgetown, Ohio, where his father owned a tannery and a farm.

The house was built in 1817 of White Allegheny pine, and the main part measures 16x19½ feet. It has a steep roof — a pitch of 5 feet. On the outside of the north end is a huge chimney servicing a spacious fireplace. The front end of the house faces Indian Creek. The interior contains a kitchen, a living room, and, at the south end, the bedroom in which Grant was born.

Location:

27 miles east of Cincinnati, Ohio at the corner of Routes 232 and 52, Cincinnati, Ohio.

OHIO

• ULYSSES S. GRANT'S BIRTHPLACE
OHIO STATE MEMORIAL
POINT PLEASANT, OHIO

ULYSSES S. GRANT'S HOME
GALENA, ILLINOIS

At the end of the Civil War, the citizens of Galena, Illinois, to demonstrate their appreciation for the achievements of their hometown war hero, General Ulysses S. Grant, presented him with this handsome home overlooking the Galena River and affording a commanding view of the city. A two-story, Italianate structure of brick, it had been built in 1859-1860 by Galena's former city clerk, Alexander J. Jackson. The house featured wide overhanging eaves supported by large wooden brackets, a low-pitched roof, white wood trim, and green shutter.

After completing his second term as President in 1877, Grant resided temporarily at Galena, but soon began an extensive world tour (1877 - 1879), after which he again stayed for a short time in the residence. After settling permanently in New York City in 1880, the Grant's rented it out until his death 5 years later.

Location:

511 Bouthillier Street, Galena, Illinois.

ULYSSES S. GRANT'S BURIAL SITE
GRANT'S TOMB
RIVERSIDE PARK, NEW YORK, NEW YORK

The National Memorial, popularly known as "Grant's Tomb", commemorates the life and career of Ulysses S. Grant and shelters the crypt containing his remains and those of his wife, Julia Dent Grant.

Shortly before his death, Grant conveyed to his son, Frederick D., a request that he be buried in New York City, where he had lived in retirement for several years. Frederick chose a picturesque location overlooking the Hudson River in newly created Riverside Park. When death came on July 23, 1885, at a cottage on Mount McGregor, near Saratogo, his father's body first lay in state at the capitol in Albany, and then was taken to New York City Hall. From there on August 8, a parade of thousands of Civil War veterans escorated it to a temporary vault in Riverside Park. The funeral, attended by the nation's highest officials, was one of the most impressive ever held in the city.

Location:

Riverside Drive and West 122nd Street, New York City, New York.

ULYSSES S. GRANT'S COTTAGE
MOUNT McGREGOR, NEW YORK

Ten miles north of Saratoga Springs, at the summit of Mount McGregor, the New York State and Recreation Division maintains Grant's Cottage, a simple little structure to which President Grant came in June 1885, seeking a cure for a cancerous throat condition.

General Grant occupied the cottage for six weeks. During these last days, he finished writing his "Personal Memoirs". He died there on July 23, 1885.

The simple furnishings of the cottage — the bed, chairs, and tables remain as they were when General Grant died. From the Lookout, to which General Grant was often wheeled in his chair, one can still view and enjoy the vast panorama of fields, rolling hills, and distant mountains to the east.

Location:

W.S. 9 north of Saratoga Springs. (follow the signs) Mount McGregor, New York.

NEW YORK

■ ULYSSES S. GRANT'S BURIAL SITE
GRANT'S TOMB
RIVERSIDE PARK NEW YORK, NEW YORK

RUTHERFORD B. HAYES
19th President

Term — March 4, 1877
to March 4, 1881

Republican Party

Birth: Delaware, Ohio. October 4, 1822.

Zodiac Sign: Libra

Ancestry: English, Scotch

Father: Rutherford Hayes. Born: Brattleboro, Vermont, January 4, 1787. Died: Delaware, Ohio, July 20, 1822.

Mother: Sophia Birchard Hayes. Born: Wilmington, Vermont, April 15, 1792. Died: Columbus, Ohio, October 30, 1866.

Brother: Lorenzo (1815 - 1825).

Sisters: Sarah Sophia (1817 - 1821). Fanny Arabella (1820 - 1856).

Wife: Lucy Ware Webb. Born: Chillicothe, Ohio, August 28, 1831. Died: Fremont, Ohio, June 25, 1889. Buried: "Spiegal Grove", Fremont, Ohio.

Marriage: Cincinnati, Ohio. December 30, 1852.

Children: Birchard Austin (1853 - 1926). Webb Cook (1856 - 1934). Rutherford Platt (1858 - 1927). Joseph (1861 - 1863). George Crook (1864 - 1866). Fanny (1867 - 1950). Scott (1871 - 1923). Manning (1873 - 1874).

Education: Academy at Norwalk, Ohio; Isaac Webb's school at Middletown, Connecticut; Kenyon College, Gambier, Ohio; Harvard Law School.

Home: Spiegal Grove, Fremont, Ohio

Religion: No specific denomination. Attended Methodist.

Occupation Before Presidency: Lawyer; soldier; politician.

Military Service: Commissioned major in 13rd Ohio Volunteers (1861); resigned as major general in June, 1865.

Pre-Presidential Offices: City Solicitor of Cincinnati, Ohio; U.S. Congressman; Governor of Ohio.

Age at Inauguration: 54

Election of 1876

(The disputed electoral votes of Florida, South Carolina, Louisiana, and Oregon were awarded to Hayes by a commission appointed by Congress.)

Candidates	Electoral Vote
Rutherford Hayes (Republican)	185
Samuel J. Tilden (Democratic)	184
Peter Cooper (Greenback)	—

The Hayes Administration

President: Rutherford B. Hayes

Vice President: William A. Wheeler of New York

Inauguration: March 3, 1877, The White House (private ceremony). March 5, 1877 — The Capitol, Washington, D.C.

Hayes took the oath of office on the steps of the east portico of the Capitol.

He was the third President who postponed their oath-taking ceremonies to Monday because March 4 fell on Sunday! However, because the election had been so vigorously disputed, he had taken the oath privately in the White House, Saturday, March 3, 1877.

Occupation After Presidency: Philanthropist; president of the National Prison Association.

President at Time of Death: Benjamin Harrison

Death: Fremont, Ohio. January 17, 1893.

Cause of Death: Heart Attack at age 70.

Place of Burial: Spiegel Grove State Park, Fremont, Ohio

"He serves his party best who serves his country best."
— Inaugural Address, 1877

**RUTHERFORD B. HAYES' BIRTHPLACE
DELAWARE, OHIO**

Rutherford B. Hayes was born in this brick house October 4, 1822, located on East William Street, a few steps east of North Sandusky Street in Delaware.

He was the son of Rutherford Hayes, a farmer, and Sophia Birchard Hayes. His father had died a few months previously. Both parents were members of families that had long lived in New England.

The house is no longer standing. The site is designated by a stone and bronze marker erected by the Delaware City Chapter of the D.A.R.

Birthplace of Rutherford B. Hayes 1822 - 1893. Lawyer, Major-General in Union Army, United States House of Representatives, Governor of Ohio and the 19th President of the United States.

Location:

East William Street, just off of Sandusky Street, Delaware, Ohio.

**RUTHERFORD B. HAYES' BIRTHPLACE
DELAWARE, OHIO**

OHIO

**• RUTHERFORD B. HAYES' BIRTHPLACE
DELAWARE, OHIO**

RUTHERFORD B. HAYES' HOME
"SPIEGEL GROVE", FREMONT, OHIO

The Spiegel Grove estate encompasses the Hayes' home, the Hayes' library and the President's tomb.

The estate was first owned by Hayes' uncle, Sardis Birchard. It was he who gave it the name Spiegel Grove; the German word "Spiegel" (mirror) suggestive of the pool of water which reflects the beauty of the trees. Rutherford B. and Lucy Webb Hayes made it their home in 1873, and inherited the house and its grounds a year later when Sardis Birchard died.

Location:

1337 Hayes Avenue at Buckland Avenue, Fremont, Ohio.

RUTHERFORD B. HAYES STATE MEMORIAL LIBRARY
FREMONT, OHIO

The Hayes Library, the first presidential library in the United States, houses more than 80,000 volumes and almost one million manuscripts. It includes a specialized library on American history from the Civil War to 1900, and is a research center for historians and writers from all over the world. The library has also preserved a large collection of personal items of the former president and his family: correspondence, diaries, scrapbooks, photographs, and paintings.

Location:

1337 Hayes Avenue at Buckland Avenue, Fremont, Ohio.

**RUTHERFORD B. HAYES' BURIAL SITE
"SPIEGEL GROVE", FREMONT, OHIO**

"Nobody ever left the Presidency with less regret than I do", Hayes said when his term ended in 1881.

Hayes returned to his home at Spiegel Grove, near Fremont, Ohio, and completely withdrew from politics. He devoted himself to philanthropic work in education, prison reform, Christianity, and veterans' affairs.

Mrs. Hayes died in June 1889. Hayes became ill while visiting friends in Cleveland in January 1893. His friends urged him to remain in bed. But Hayes insisted on returning home, saying, "I would rather die at Spiegel Grove than to live anywhere else." He died on January 17, 1893. His last words were: "I know I am going where Lucy is."

The president's tomb is located on a quiet knoll in the grove of trees south of the house. The trail that runs through the grove nearby the tomb was once part of the famous Indian trail which ran from Lake Erie to the Ohio River.

Near the trail is a monument of Vermont granite marking the final resting place of President and Mrs. Hayes.
Location:
1337 Hayes Avenue at Buckland Avenue, Fremont, Ohio.

**■ RUTHERFORD B. HAYES' BURIAL SITE
"SPIEGEL GROVE", FREMONT, OHIO**

JAMES A. GARFIELD
20th President

Term — March 4, 1881 to September 19, 1881

Republican Party

Birth: Orange Township, Ohio. November 19, 1831.

Zodiac Sign: Scorpio

Ancestry: English and French

Father: Abram Garfield. Born: Worcester, New York, December 28, 1799. Died: Orange Township, Ohio, May 8, 1833.

Mother: Eliza Ballou Garfield. Born: Richmond, New Hampshire, September 21, 1801. Died: Mentor, Ohio, January 21, 1888.

Brothers: Thomas (1822 - ?). James Ballou (1826 - 1829).

Sisters: Mehitabel (1821 - ?). Mary (1824 - 1884).

Wife: Lucretia Rudolph. Born: Hiram, Ohio, April 19, 1832. Died: Pasadena, California, March 14, 1918. Buried: Lake View Cemetery, Cleveland, Ohio.

Marriage: Hiram, Ohio. November 11, 1858.

Children: Eliza Arabella (1860 - 1863). Harry Augustus (1863 - 1942). James Rudolph (1865 - 1950). Mary (1867 - 1947). Irin McDowell (1870 - 1951). Abram (1872 - 1958). Edward (1874 - 1876).

Education: Attended Geauga Academy and Western Reserve Eclectic Institute; graduated (1856) from Williams College.

Home: "Lawnfield", Mentor, Ohio

Religion: Disciples of Christ

Occupation Before Presidency: School-teacher; soldier; president of Hiram College.

Military Service: Commissioned lt. col. of 42nd Ohio Volunteers in August (1861); rose to brig. gen. of Volunteers (1862), and maj. gen. of Volunteers (1863).

Pre-Presidential Offices: Member of Ohio Senate; Member of U.S. House of Representatives; Chairman of House Committee on Appropriations; Minority Leader in U.S. House of Representatives.

Political Party: Republican

Age of Inauguration: 49

Election of 1880

Candidates	Electoral Vote
James A. Garfield (Republican)	214
Winfield S. Hancock (Democratic)	115
James B. Weaver (Greenback - Labor)	—
Neal Dow (Prohibition)	—

The Garfield Administration

President: James A. Garfield

Vice President: Chester A. Arthur of New York

Inauguration: March 4, 1881

The Capitol, Washington, D.C.

Death: Elberon, New Jersey. September 19, 1881.

Cause of Death: Assassination at age 49. July 2, 1881, shot by Charles J. Guiteau in Baltimore and Potomac railroad station, Washington, D.C.

Place of Burial: Lake View Cemetery, Cleveland, Ohio.

"Next in importance to freedom and justice is popular education, without which neither freedom nor justice can be premanently maintained."
— Letter Accepting Presidential Nomination, 1880

JAMES A. GARFIELD'S BIRTHPLACE
MENTOR, OHIO

James Abram Garfield was born in Cuyahogo County (Orange township) now Moreland Hills, Ohio on November 19, 1831, in a rough log cabin whose chinks were filled with mud to keep out the winter winds. The windows were of greased paper; the furniture was crude and simple.

His father, Abram Garfield, spent his boyhood in New York State, later moving to the Western Reserve. Here in the new lands he was happy to meet Eliza Ballou, who had been his childhood playmate in New York; the two were soon married, and to them was born a son, two daughters, and another son — the last, named James, destined to the highest office in the land.

The replica log cabin birthplace is located on the gounds of the James A. Garfield Home (Lawnfield) Mentor, Ohio.

Location:
    8095 Mentor Avenue, Mentor, Ohio.

OHIO

• JAMES A. GARFIELD'S BIRTHPLACE
MORELAND, OHIO

83

**JAMES A. GARFIELD'S HOME
"LAWNFIELD", MENTOR, OHIO**

Late in the fall of 1876, James Garfield bought the old Dickey farm in Mentor. He was then 45 years of age and the U.S. Representative from the 19th District of Ohio.

From 1877 to 1880, when Garfield was elected the 20th President of the United States, the Mentor farm occupied much of his attention.

The 1½ story farmhouse was remodeled in three stages, and grew from six or seven rooms to a spacious mansion of 26 rooms.

The Lake County Historical Society maintains the interior of the home and its grounds. Visitors to the home can see the personal possessions of the Garfield family, including the White House china and the inaugural Bible. The lovely brass light ceiling fixtures are the originals, once gas but now electric.

The magnificent library of handcarved white oak, installed a few years after the President's death to house his journals and papers, is the outstanding feature of the home. The visitor can observe from the vast collection of books how varied and well-founded were Garfield's interests — technical, classical, spiritual and humorous.

Immediately surrounding the home are over a hundred trees of many varieties, exotic as well as native, most of which were planted by the President and Mrs. Garfield.

Location:

8095 Mentor Avenue, Mentor, Ohio.

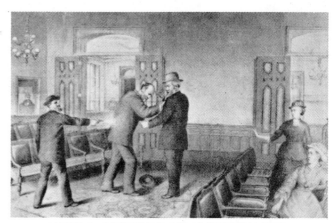

**JAMES A. GARFIELD'S ASSASSINATION SITE
BALTIMORE AND POTOMAC RAILROAD STATION
WASHINGTON, D.C.**

On July 2, 1881, less than four months after Garfield's inauguration, a demented office seeker named Charles J. Guiteau, fired two shots at the President as he stood with Secretary of State Blaine in the Baltimore and Potomac depot in Washington. One shot grazed the President's arm; the other entered his back, fracturing the spine. The assassin was quickly collared and taken off to jail. In the weeks that followed, as the President lay suffering in the White House, well wishers brought a variety of medicines.

Alexander Graham Bell was summoned to the White House to find the exact location of the bullet by means of his induction-balance device. The President lingered on through the hot summer. On September 6 he was moved in a special train to the seaside town of Elberon, New Jersey, where his wife constantly attended him and prepared all his meals. Garfield seemed to be recovering until September 19, when he awoke with a chill and grew progressively weaker. He died that night at 10:30 p.m.

Location:

Baltimore and Potomac Railroad Station, Washington, D.C.

**JAMES A. GARFIELD'S BURIAL SITE
GARFIELD MONUMENT
LAKE VIEW CEMETERY, CLEVELAND, OHIO**

The Garfield Monument, located on a commanding hill in Lake View Cemetery, is a circular tower 50 feet in diameter and 180 feet high, built of native Ohio sandstone upon a broad stone terrace. A square stone porch projects at the base of the tower; around the exterior of the porch are five panels in bas-relief depicting Garfield's life and death.

The center of the monument is the Memorial Hall, which takes the full area of the tower's base. In it is a statue of Garfield just risen to speak in Congress. The sculpture is by Alexander Doyle, who obtained his marble from the famed quarries near Carrara, Italy, which were first opened by Leonardo da Vinci. In the crypt directly below the Memorial Hall are the bronze casket of Garfield, draped with an American flag, and that of his wife, Lucretia Garfield, who died 37 years after his assassination.

Location:

12316 Euclid Avenue at 123rd Street, Cleveland, Ohio.

**JAMES A. GARFIELD'S BURIAL SITE
GARFIELD MONUMENT
LAKE VIEW CEMETERY, CLEVELAND, OHIO**

OHIO

**■ JAMES A. GARFIELD'S BURIAL SITE
GARFIELD MONUMENT
LAKE VIEW CEMETERY, CLEVELAND, OHIO**

CHESTER A. ARTHUR
21st President

**Term — September 20, 1881
to March 4, 1885**

Republican Party

Birth: Fairfield, Vermont. October 5, 1830.
Zodiac Sign: Libra
Ancestry: Scotch - Irish and English
Father: William Arthur. Born: County Antrim, Ireland, December 5, 1796. Died: Newtonville, New York, October 27, 1875.
Mother: Malvina Stone Arthur. Born: Berkshire, Vermont. April 24, 1802. Died: Newtonville, New York, January 16, 1869.
Brothers: William (1834 - 1915). George (1836 - 1838)
Sisters: Regina (1822 - 1910). Jane (1824 - 1842). Almeda (1826 - 1899). Ann Eliza (1828 - 1915). Malvina (1832 - 1920). Mary (1841 - 1917).
Wife: Ellen Lewis Herndon. Born: Fredericksburg, Virginia, August 30, 1837. Died: New York, New York, January 12, 1880. Buried: Albany Rural Cemetery, Albany, New York
Marriage: New York, New York. October 25, 1859.
Children: William Lewis Herndon (1860 - 1863). Chester Alan Jr. (1864 - 1937). Ellen (1871 - 1915).
Education: Attended public schools and Lyceum School; graduated with honors from Union College (1848).
Religion: Episcopalian
Occupation Before Presidency: Teacher; school principal; lawyer.
Pre-Presidential Offices: Quartermaster General of New York State; New York Collector of Customs; Vice President of the U.S.
Political Party: Republican
Age at Inauguration: 50
Note: The fourth Vice President who succeeded to the Presidency because of the death of his predecessor, James Garfield.
The Arthur Administration
President: Chester A. Arthur
Inauguration: September 20, 1881
New York, New York

Occupation After Presidency: Retired
President at Time of Death: Grover Cleveland
Death: New York City, New York. November 18, 1886.
Cause of Death: Bright's disease, cerebral hemorrhage at age 56.
Place of Burial: Rural Cemetery, Albany, New York.

"No higher or more assuring proof could exist of the strength and permanence of popular government than the fact that though the chosen of the people be struct down, his Constitutional successor is peacefully installed without shock or strain."

— Inaugural Address, 1881

**CHESTER A. ARTHUR'S BIRTHPLACE
FAIRFIELD, VERMONT**

**• CHESTER A. ARTHUR'S BIRTHPLACE
FAIRFIELD, VERMONT**

**CHESTER A. ARTHUR'S BIRTHPLACE
FAIRFIELD, VERMONT**

The birth of Chester A. Arthur, 21st President of the United States, on October 5, 1830, took place in a modest one-story clapboard house on a remote ledge hillside northeast of Fairfield Station. The house has long since disappeared.

His father, William, had come to America from Northern Ireland. Chester's mother, Malvina Stone Arthur, grew up on her father's Vermont farm.

At the age of 18, Arthur was graduated from Union College in Schenectody, New York. He began studying law and at the same time taught school. He joined a New York City law firm in 1853. Arthur soon became known as a defender of Negro civil rights.

Location:

A replica of Arthur's birthplace is about 3½ miles east of Fairfield Station on the road that leads to State Route 108. Fairfield, Vermont.

**CHESTER A. ARTHUR'S BURIAL SITE
RURAL CEMETERY, ALBANY, NEW YORK**

Chester Arthur resumed his law practice in New York City after he had been President, but a heart ailment soon forced him to retire. He died of a cerebral hemorrhage on November 18, 1886. He was buried beside his wife in the Rural Cemetery at Albany, New York.

Location:

Cemetery Avenue off Broadway, Menands, New York.

**■ CHESTER A. ARTHUR'S BURIAL SITE
RURAL CEMETERY, ALBANY, NEW YORK**

GROVER CLEVELAND
22nd and 24th President

Term — March 5, 1885
to March 4, 1889

Term — March 4, 1893
to March 4, 1897

Democratic Party

Birth: Caldwell, New Jersey. March 18, 1837.

Zodiac Sign: Pisces

Ancestry: Irish - English

Father: Richard Falley Cleveland. Born: Norwich, Connecticut, June 19, 1804. Died: Holland Patent, New York, October 1, 1853.

Mother: Ann Neal Cleveland. Born: Baltimore, Maryland, February 4, 1806. Died: Holland Patent, New York, July 19, 1882.

Brothers: William Neal (1832 - 1906). Richard Cecil (1835 - 1872). Lewis Frederick (1841 - 1872).

Sisters: Anna Neal (1830 - 1909). Mary Allen (1833 - 1914). Margaret Louise (1838 - 1932). Susan Sophia (1843 - ?). Rose (1846 - 1918).

Wife: Frances Folsom. Born: Buffalo, New York, July 21, 1864. Died: Baltimore, Maryland, October 29, 1947. Buried: Princeton Cemetery, Princeton, New Jersey.

Marriage: Washington, D.C. June 2, 1886. (White House)

Children: Ruth (1891 - 1904). Esther (1893 -   ). Marion (1895 -   ). Richard Folsom (1897 - 1974). Francis Grover (1903 -   ).

Education: Public Schools

Religion: Presbyterian

Occupation Before Presidency: Lawyer

Pre-Presidential Offices: Erie County Assistant District Attorney; Sheriff of Erie County; Mayor of Buffalo; Governor of New York

Age at Inauguration: 47

Occupation After Presidency: Princeton University Trustee.

Election of 1884

Candidates	Electoral Vote
Grover Cleveland (Democratic)	219
James G. Blaine (Republican)	182
Benjamin F. Butler (Greenback - Labor)	—
John P. St. John (Prohibition)	—

First Administration

President: Grover Cleveland
Vice President: Thomas A. Hendricks of Indiana
Inauguration: March 4, 1885
The Capitol, Washington, D.C.

Election of 1892

Candidates	Electoral Vote
Grover Cleveland (Democratic)	277
Benjamin Harrison (Republican)	145
James B. Weaver (People's)	22
John Bedwell (Prohibition)	—
Simon Wing (Socialist Labor)	—

Second Administration

President: Grover Cleveland
Vice President: Adlai E. Stevenson of Illinois
Inauguration: March 4, 1893
The Capitol, Washington, D.C.

Occupation After Presidency: Princeton University Trustee.

President at Time of Death: Theodore Roosevelt

Death: Princeton, New Jersey. June 24, 1908.

Cause of Death: Heart attack at age 71.

Place of Burial: Princeton Cemetery, Princeton, New Jersey.

"Your every voter, as surely as your chief magistrate, exercises a public trust."

— Inaugural Address, 1885

GROVER CLEVELAND'S BIRTHPLACE
CALDWELL, NEW JERSEY

Stephen Grover Cleveland was born on March 18, 1837, in Caldwell, New Jersey. He dropped his first name while still a boy. Grover was the fifth child in a family of four brothers and five sisters. His father, Richard Folley Cleveland, was a Presbyterian minister and a relative of Moses Cleveland, the founder of Cleveland, Ohio. His mother, Ann Neal Cleveland was the daughter of a publisher.

Cleveland's birthplace was the manse of the First Presbyterian Church of Caldwell, New Jersey, built in 1832. Grover Cleveland, the minister's son, was born in the rear room of the first floor, and lived here from 1837 to 1840. The clapboard house has been preserved as a museum.

Location:

207 Bloomfield Avenue, Caldwell, New Jersey.

GROVER CLEVELAND'S BIRTHPLACE
CALDWELL, NEW JERSEY

NEW

JERSEY

• GROVER CLEVELAND'S BIRTHPLACE
CALDWELL, NEW JERSEY

GROVER CLEVELAND'S HOME
"WESTLAND", PRINCETON, NEW JERSEY

Westland was the home of Grover Cleveland from the time of his retirement from the Presidency in 1897 until his death in 1908.

Cleveland named the house "Westland" in honor of his close friend and professor at Princeton University, Andrew F. West.

"Westland", privately owned and in excellent condition, is closed to the public.

Location:

15 Hodge Road, Princeton, New Jersey.

■ **GROVER CLEVELAND'S BURIAL SITE**
PRINCETON CEMETERY
PRINCETON, NEW JERSEY

GROVER CLEVELAND'S BURIAL SITE
PRINCETON CEMETERY, PRINCETON, NEW JERSEY

Grover Cleveland spent his last years in Princeton, New Jersey. He served Princeton University as lecturer and as a trustee. After a three month illness, Cleveland died on June 24, 1908. His last words were: "I have tried so hard to do right."

To the north, toward Witherspoon Street in Princeton Cemetery is this monument and burial site of Grover Cleveland, the 22nd and 24th President of the United States, who lived in Princeton from 1897 to 1908. Each year, on his birthday, a wreath from the White House is laid at his grave.

Location:

Whitherspoon and Wiggins Streets, Princeton, New Jersey.

BENJAMIN HARRISON
23rd President

Term — March 4, 1889
to March 4, 1893

Republican Party

Birth: North Bend, Ohio. August 20, 1833.

Zodiac Sign: Leo

Ancestry: English - Scotch

Father: John Scott Harrison. Born: Vincennes, Indiana, October 4, 1804. Died: North Bend, Ohio, May 25, 1878.

Mother: Elizabeth Irwin Harrison. Born: Mercersburg, Pennsylvania, July 18, 1810. Died: Probably North Bend, Ohio, August 15, 1850.

Brothers: Archibald Irwin (1832 - 1870). Carter Bassett (1840 - 1905). John Scott Jr. (1844 - 1926). James Friedlay (1847 - 1848).

Sisters: Mary Jane Irwin (1835 - 1867). Anna Symmes (1842 - 1926).

Half Sisters: Elizabeth Short (1825 - 1904). Sarah Lucretia (1829 - ?).

First Wife: Caroline (Carrie) Lavinia Scott. Born: Oxford, Ohio, October 1, 1832. Died: Washington, D.C., October 25, 1892. Buried: Crown Hill Cemetery, Indianapolis, Indiana.

First Marriage: Oxford, Ohio. October 20, 1853.

Children: Russell Benjamin (1854 - 1936). Mary Scott (1858 - 1930).

Second Wife: Mary Scott Lord Dimmick. Born: Honesdale, Pennsylvania, April 30, 1858. Died: New York, New York, January 5, 1948. Buried: Crown Hill Cemetery, Indianapolis, Indiana.

Second Marriage: New York, New York. April 6, 1896.

Children: Elizabeth (1897 - 1955).

Education: Private tutoring; attended Farmers College; graduated B.A. (1852) from Miami University.

Religion: Presbyterian

Home: Indianapolis, Indiana

Occupation Before Presidency: Lawyer; notary public; soldier.

Military Service: Appointed col. in 70th Indiana Volunteers (1862); resigned as brevet brig. gen. in 1865.

Pre-Presidential Offices: Commissioner for the Court of Claims; City Attorney; Secretary of Indiana Republican Central Committee; State Supreme Court Reporter; Member of the U.S. Senate.

Political Party: Republican

Age at Inauguration: 55

Election of 1888

Candidates	Electoral Vote
Benjamin Harrison (Republican)	233
Grover Cleveland (Democratic)	168
Clinton B. Fisk (Prohibition)	—

The Harrison Administration

President: Benjamin Harrison

Vice President: Levi P. Morton of New York

Inauguration: March 4, 1889

The Capitol, Washington, D.C.

Occupation After Presidency: Lawyer

President at Time of Death: William McKinley

Death: Indianapolis, Indiana. March 13, 1901.

Cause of Death: Pneumonia at age 67.

Place of Burial: Crown Hill Cemetery, Indianapolis, Indiana.

"Let those who would die for the flag on the field of battle give a better proof of their patroistism and a higher glory to their country by promoting fraternity and justice."

— Inaugural Address, 1889

**BENJAMIN HARRISON'S BIRTHPLACE
"THE BIG HOUSE", NORTH BEND, OHIO**

**BENJAMIN HARRISON'S HOME
INDIANAPOLIS, INDIANA**

Benjamin Harrison was born August 20, 1833, on his grandfather's estate at North Bend, Ohio. He was named for his great-grandfather, a signer of the Declaration of Independence. Ben was the second of nine children of John Scott Harrison and Elizabeth Irwin Harrison. Ben, a short stocky boy, spent his youth on the farm. Harrison attended Farmers' College in a Cincinnati suburb for three years. He graduated from Miami University in 1852. After reading law with a Cincinnati firm, Harrison was admitted to the bar in 1854. He moved to Indianapolis that same year.

Harrison's birthplace, a red brick home in North Bend, Ohio, was torn down in 1959. It was located on the southwest corner of Symmes Avenue and Washington Avenue.

Location:

15 miles west of Cincinnati, on U.S. Hwy. 50 to North Bend, Ohio.

**• BENJAMIN HARRISON'S BIRTHPLACE
"THE BIG HOUSE", NORTH BEND, OHIO**

93

BENJAMIN HARRISON'S HOME
INDIANAPOLIS, INDIANA

BENJAMIN HARRISON'S BURIAL SITE
CROWN HILL CEMETERY, INDIANAPOLIS, INDIANA

Benjamin Harrison, 23rd President of the United States, lived in this house from the 1870's until his death in 1901.

As you wander leisurely through this lovely nineteenth century home just as it was when Benjamin Harrison lived here from 1874 to 1901 — you will find yourself carried back to a bygone era, which began almost a century ago. And as you look at Benjamin Harrison's personal possessions, his books and mementos of his career, you will feel a warm, almost personal closeness to the man, himself.

To him we owe the formation of our huge National Park System and the conservation and preservation of the great redwoods of California, and the daily display of the American flag over public buildings.

Location:

1230 North Delaware Street, Indianapolis, Indiana.

Benjamin Harrison returned to Indianapolis and the practice of law. In 1897, he wrote "This Country of Ours", a book about the federal government. Benjamin Harrison died at his home on March 13, 1901, and was buried at Crown Hill Cemetery in Indianapolis, Indiana.

One of the world's largest, most beautiful, and best cared-for cemetery, Crown Hill belongs to all the people of the community.

Location:

700 West 38th Street, Indianapolis, Indiana.

■ BENJAMIN HARRISON'S BURIAL SITE
CROWN HILL CEMETERY
INDIANAPOLIS, INDIANA

WILLIAM McKINLEY
25th President

**Term — March 4, 1897
to March 4, 1901**

Republican Party

Birth: Niles, Ohio. January 29, 1843
Zodiac Sign: Aquarius
Ancestry: Scotch - Irish and English
Father: William McKinley. Born: Mercer County, Pennsylvania, November 15, 1807. Died: Canton, Ohio, November 24, 1892.
Mother: Nancy Cambell Allison McKinley. Born: New Lisbon, Ohio, April 22, 1809. Died: Canton, Ohio, December 12, 1897.
Brothers: David Allison (1829 - 1892). James (? - 1889). Abner (1849 - 1904).
Sisters: Anna (1832 - 1890). Mary, Helen, Sarah Elizabeth.
Wife: Ida Saxton. Born: Canton, Ohio, June 8, 1847. Died: Canton, Ohio, May 26, 1907. Buried: McKinley Tomb, Canton, Ohio.
Marriage: Canton, Ohio. January 25, 1871.
Children: Katherine (1871 - 1875). Ida (1873 - 1873).
Education: Attended Poland Acadamy, Ohio; Allegheny College, Meadville, Pennsylvania.
Religion: Methodist
Occupation Before Presidency: Teacher; soldier; lawyer.
Military Service: Joined Ohio 23rd Volunteers in 1861; rose to rank of major before leaving Army in 1865.
Pre-Presidential Offices: Member of U.S. House of Representatives; Governor of Ohio.
Age at Inauguration: 54
Election of 1896

Candidates	Electoral Vote
William McKinley (Republican)	271
William J. Bryan (Democratic)	176
John M. Palmer (National Democratic)	—
Joshua Levering (Prohibition)	—

First Administration
President: William McKinley
Vice President: Garret A. Hobart of New Jersey
Inauguration: March 4, 1897
The Capitol, Washington, D.C.
Election of 1900

Candidates	Electoral Vote
William McKinley (Republican)	292
William J. Bryan (Democratic)	155
John C. Wooley (Prohibition)	—
Eugene V. Debs (Socialist)	—

Second Administration
President: William McKinley
Vice President: Theodore Roosevelt of New York
Inauguration: March 4, 1901
The Capitol, Washington, D.C.
Death: Buffalo, New York. September 14, 1901.
Cause of Death: Assassination at age 58. September 6, 1901, shot by Leon F. Czolgosz in Temple of Music, Pan-American Exposition, Buffalo, New York.
Place of Burial: McKinley State Memorial and Tomb, Canton, Ohio.

"We want no war or conquest . . . War Should never be entered upon until every agency of peace has failed."
— Inaugural Address, 1897

WILLIAM McKINLEY'S BIRTHPLACE
WILLIAM McKINLEY'S PLAQUE
LOCATED IN McKINLEY FEDERAL SAVINGS AND LOAN
NILES, OHIO

WILLIAM McKINLEY'S BIRTHPLACE
NILES, OHIO

• WILLIAM McKINLEY'S BIRTHPLACE
NILES, OHIO

William McKinley was born on January 29, 1843, in Niles, Ohio. A country store occupied part of the first floor of the long, two story family home. McKinley's father, also named William, and his mother, Nancy McKinley, were of Scotch - Irish ancestry. William, first attended school in Niles. When he was nine years old, his parents decided that the school was not adequate. He entered the Poland Seminary, a private school. At 17, McKinley entered the junior class of Allegheny College in Meadville, Pennsylvania. Severe illness soon forced him to return home. He later taught briefly in a country school.

The house was bought by a Mr. Wess and moved to McKinley Heights, where it was operated as a private museum until it was destroyed by fire about 1935.

The McKinley Federal Savings and Loan Association building now occupies the site where William McKinley was born.

As you enter the door to the McKinley Federal Savings and Loan, a plaque of William McKinley is located on the left side of the building.

Location:

36 South Main Street, U.S. Hwy. 422, Niles, Ohio.

96

**WILLIAM McKINLEY'S HOME
CANTON, OHIO**

"Front Porch" Campaign 1896.

McKinley remained at his home in Canton, Ohio during his presidential campaigns and gave rehearsed speeches. He refused to leave his invalid wife for tours about the country.

The home has been destroyed.

Location:

Across the street from the McKinley High School. 9th and Market North, Canton, Ohio.

**WILLIAM McKINLEY'S ASSASSINATION SITE
BUFFALO, NEW YORK**

McKinley delivered one of the most important speeches of his career at the Pan-American Exposition in Buffalo, New York, on September 5, 1901.

The next day he held a public reception in the exposition's Temple of Music. Hundreds of people waited to shake his hand. They included an American born Polish anarchist named Leon F. Czolgosz. As he drew near, Czolgosz extended his left hand to grasp McKinley's outstretched hand. Czolgosz fired two bullets into the President's body with a revolver concealed by a handkerchief in his right hand. McKinley slumped forward, gasping, "Am I shot?" The crowd pounced on the assassin and began beating him. McKinley pointed to Czolgosz, imploring, "Let no one hurt him". He whispered to his secretary, "My wife — be careful, Cortelyou, how you tell her — oh, be careful". An ambulance rushed the wounded President to a hospital for emergency surgery. For a time. McKinley appeared to be recovering, but he died on September 14, 1901. Czolgosz, who had confessed a great urge to kill a "great ruler", was later electrocuted.

A bronze tablet set in a rock in Fordham Drive marks the site where McKinley was shot.

Location:

Near Lincoln Parkway, Buffalo, New York.

**WILLIAM McKINLEY MEMORIAL LIBRARY
NILES, OHIO**

This building, an excellent example of Greek classic architecture, was constructed as a memorial to the twenty-fifth President of the United States, William McKinley, who was born in Niles, Ohio.

The building consists of a Court of Honor flanked by two lateral wings, one of which is designed as an assembly room and the other a library.

The second floor is reached by a marble stairway, and here are placed the memorabilia of McKinley and historical relics of all kinds associated with the part he played in the nation's history, in both peace and war.

Location:

Main Street, Niles, Ohio.

97

**WILLIAM McKINLEY'S BURIAL SITE
WESTLAND CEMETERY, CANTON, OHIO**

Thousands of people from all over the world visit the McKinley National Memorial in Canton every year. It was erected in 1907, paid for by pennies contributed by school children of all over the United States, to honor the **Cantonian** whose second term as the 25th President was cut down be an assassin's bullet on September 6, 1901, at the Pan-American Exposition in Buffalo, New York.

A Memorial to Our Martyred President — McKinley Monument, dedicated September 30, 1907, is the final resting place of William McKinley, 25th President of the United States. Also interred here are his wife, Ida Saxton McKinley, and their two infant children, Ida and Katie.

Location:

McKinley Tomb, Westland Cemetery, 7th Street N.W., Canton, Ohio.

**WILLIAM McKINLEY'S BURIAL SITE
WESTLAND CEMETERY, CANTON, OHIO**

OHIO

**■ WILLIAM McKINLEY'S BURIAL SITE
WESTLAND CEMETERY, CANTON, OHIO**

THEODORE ROOSEVELT
26th President

Term — September 14, 1901
to March 4, 1909

Republican Party

Theodore Roosevelt

Birth: New York, New York. October 27, 1858
Zodiac Sign: Scorpio
Ancestry: Dutch, Scotch, English, Huguenot
Father: Theodore Roosevelt. Born: New York, New York, September 22, 1831. Died: New York, New York, February 9, 1878.
Mother: Martha Bulloch Roosevelt. Born: Roswell, Georgia, July 8, 1834. Died: New York, New York, February 14, 1884.
Brother: Elliott (1860 - 1894).
Sisters: Anna (1855 - 1931). Corinne (1861 - 1933).
First Wife: Alice Hathoway Lee. Born: Chestnut Hill, Massachusetts, July 29, 1861. Died: New York, New York, February 14, 1884. Buried: Cambridge, Massachusetts.
First Marriage: Brookline, Massachusetts. October 27, 1880.
Children: Alice Lee (1884 - 1981).
Second Wife: Edith Kermit Carow. Born: Norwich, Connecticut, August 6, 1861. Died: Oyster Bay, New York, September 30, 1948. Buried: Young Memorial Cemetery, Oyster Bay, New York.
Second Marriage: London, England. December 2, 1886.
Children: Theodore (1887 - 1944). Kermit (1889 - 1943). Ethel Carow (1891 - 1977). Archibald (1894 - 1979). Quentin (1897 - 1918).
Education: Private tutoring; B.A. from Harvard; studied law at Columbia.
Religion: Reformed Dutch
Homes: 28 East 20th Street, New York, New York. "Sagamore Hill", Oyster Bay, New York.
Occupation Before Presidency: Writer; historian; politician.
Military Service: Lt. colonel, colonel, First U.S. Volunteer Cavalry Regiment ("Rough Riders"), 1898.

Pre-Presidential Offices: New York State Assemblyman; U.S. Civil Service Commissioner; President of New York Board of Police Commissioners; Assistant Secretary of the Navy; Governor of New York; Vice President of the U.S.
Political Party: Republican; ran on Progressive ticket in 1912.
Age at Inauguration: 42
Note: The fifth Vice President who succeeded to the Presidency because of the death of his predecessor, William McKinley.
The First Administration
President: Theodore Roosevelt
Inauguration: September 14, 1901
Buffalo, New York
Election of 1904

Candidates	Electoral Vote
Theodore Roosevelt (Republican)	336
Alton B. Parker (Democratic)	140
Eugene V. Debs (Socialist)	—
Silas C. Swallow (Prohibition)	—
Thomas E. Watson (People's)	—

The Second Administration
President: Theodore Roosevelt
Vice President: Charles Warren Fairbanks of Indiana
Inauguration: March 4, 1905
The Capitol, Washington, D.C.
Occupation After Presidency: Writer; politician.
President at Time of Death: Woodrow Wilson
Death: Oyster Bay, New York. January 6, 1919.
Cause of Death: Embolism in coronary artery at age 60.
Place of Burial: Young's Memorial Cemetery, Oyster Bay, New York.

"It is well indeed for our land that we of this generation have learned to think nationally."
— Builders of The State

THEODORE ROOSEVELT'S BIRTHPLACE
NEW YORK, NEW YORK

THEODORE ROOSEVELT'S BIRTHPLACE
NEW YORK, NEW YORK

Theodore Roosevelt was born in New York City on October 27, 1858. He was the second of the four children of Theodore and Martha Bulloch Roosevelt. "Teddie" as the family called him, was a weak, sickly child. His father installed a gymnasium in the house, and the boy exercised there regularly.

Theodore loved both books and the outdoors. He combined these interests in nature study. He went with his family on year-long trips abroad. Roosevelt studied under tutors until he entered Harvard University in 1876 at the age of 18. Roosevelt was graduated from Harvard in 1880.

A typical Victorian brownstone, it contains many items relating to Roosevelt's career and travels.

Location:
    28 East 20th Street, New York, New York.

• THEODORE ROOSEVELT'S BIRTHPLACE
NEW YORK, NEW YORK

ROOSEVELT NATIONAL MEMORIAL PARK
MALTESE CROSS CABIN
MEDORA, NORTH DAKOTA

After the death of his wife and mother in 1884, Roosevelt left politics. He bought two cattle ranches on the Little Missouri River in the Dakota Territory. The hard life and endless activity of a rancher helped him recover from his sorrow. Wearing cowboy clothes, Roosevelt often spent 14 to 16 hours a day in the saddle. He hunted buffalo and other wild animals, tended cattle, and even helped law officers capture a band of outlaws. Severe snowstorms in the winter of 1885-1886 destroyed most of Roosevelt's cattle. He returned to New York City in 1886.

Motorists entering the South Unit of the park at the Medora entrance should first stop at the visitor center, which features exhibits on the history and natural history of the park. To the north of the center is the Maltese Cross Cabin.

Location:

Interstate I-94 at Medora, North Dakota.

THEODORE ROOSEVELT'S HOME
"SAGAMORE HILL", OYSTER BAY,
LONG ISLAND, NEW YORK

"Sagamore Hill", overlooking Oyster Bay Harbor and Long Island Sound, was the home of Theodore Roosevelt for nearly four decades and is the site most closely associated with his life and career. During the period, 1901 to 1909, as a "summer White House", it was the focus of national attention and the scene of numerous major events and decisions. Today, the little-altered mansion, furnished with Roosevelt's possessions, is one of the most authentically preserved historic sites in the nation.

The wide plaza on the south and west sides of the house figured prominently in daily life at the estate, but was also on three occasions the scene of notable historical events. On it Roosevelt received official notification of his nominations for the governorship of New York in 1898, for Vice President in 1900, and for the Presidency in 1904.

Location:

3 miles N.E. of Oyster Bay, Long Island on Cove Neck Road, Oyster Bay, New York.

**THEODORE ROOSEVELT'S BURIAL SITE
YOUNG MEMORIAL CEMETERY, OYSTER BAY, NEW YORK**

After leaving the Presidency in March 1909, Roosevelt sailed for Africa to hunt big game. He and his party brought down 296 big-game animals, including 9 lions.

In 1913 and 1914, Roosevelt had explored the River of Doubt in the Brazilian jungle. He contacted a form of jungle fever, and returned weak and prematurely aged. Early in 1918, Roosevelt underwent operations to remove obscesses on his thigh and in his ears.

Theodore Roosevelt died unexpectedly of a blood clot in the heart on January 6, 1919. He was buried at Young Memorial Cemetery, Oyster Bay, New York. His first wife had been buried in New York City. His second wife died in 1948 and was buried beside him in Oyster Bay.

Location:

1 mile east on Main Street, Oyster Bay, Long Island, New York.

NEW YORK

■ **THEODORE ROOSEVELT'S BURIAL SITE
YOUNG MEMORIAL CEMETERY
OYSTER BAY, NEW YORK**

WILLIAM HOWARD TAFT
27th President

Term — March 4, 1909
to March 4, 1913

Republican Party

Birth: Cincinnati, Ohio. September 15, 1857
Zodiac Sign: Virgo
Ancestry: English; Scotch - Irish
Father: Alphonso Taft. Born: Townshend, Vermont, November 5, 1810. Died: San Diego, California, May 21, 1891.
Mother: Louise Torrey Taft. Born: Boston, Massachusetts, September 11, 1827. Died: Millbury, Massachusetts, December 7, 1907.
Brothers: Henry Waters (1859 - 1945). Horace Dutton (1861 - 1943).
Sister: Frances (1865 - 1950).
Half Brothers: Charles Phelps (1843 - 1929). Rawson (1845 - 1889).
Wife: Hellen (Nellie) Herron. Born: Cincinnati, Ohio, June 2, 1861. Died: Washington, D.C., May 22, 1943. Buried: Arlington National Cemetery, Arlington, Virginia
Marraige: Cincinnati, Ohio. June 19, 1886.
Children: Robert Alphonso (1889 - 1953). Helen (1891 -). Charles Phelps II (1897 - 1917).
Education: Woodward Hill School, Cincinnati, Ohio; B.A. from Yale University; Cincinnati Law School.
Religion: Unitarian
Occupation Before Presidency: Lawyer; judge.
Pre-Presidential Offices: Assistant Prosecuting Attorney, Hamilton County, Ohio; Ohio Superior Court Judge; U.S. Solicitor General; Federal Circuit Court Judge; Civil Governor of Philippines; Secretary of War.
Age at Inauguration: 51
Election of 1908

Candidates	Electoral Vote
William H. Taft (Republican)	321
William J. Bryan (Democratic)	162
Eugene V. Debs (Socialist)	—
Eugene W. Chafin (Prohibition)	—
Thomas L. Hisgen (Independence)	—

The Taft Administration
President: William Howard Taft
Vice President: James S. Sherman of New York
Inauguration: March 4, 1909
House of Representatives, Washington, D.C.
Occupation After Presidency: Kent professor of Constitutional law — Yale University; joint chairman of National War Labor Board; Chief Justice of U.S. Supreme Court.
President at Time of Death: Herbert C. Hoover
Death: Washington D.C. March 8, 1930.
Cause of Death: Debility at age 72.
Place of Burial: Arlington National Cemetery, Washington, D.C.

"A government is for the benefit of all the people . . ."
— Veto of Arizona Enabling Act, 1911

**WILLIAM HOWARD TAFT'S HOME
"THE QUARRY", CINCINNATI, OHIO**

William Taft and his wife, "Nellie" Herron, moved to this home in 1886, the year they were married.

Subsequently, his political career necessitated his relocation to Washington, D.C.

Privately owned. Not open to the public.
Location:
1763 East McMillan Street, Cincinnati, Ohio.

**WILLIAM HOWARD TAFT'S BIRTHPLACE AND
BOYHOOD HOME, CINCINNATI, OHIO**

William Howard Taft was born on September 15, 1857. He was the second son of Alphonso Taft and his second wife, Louise Maria Torrey Taft. Will Taft was a large, fair, attractive youth. They called him "Big Lub" because of his size. At 17 he enrolled in Yale College. In 1878, Taft was graduated second in his class. He then studied law at the Cincinnati Law School. He received his law degree in 1880 and was admitted to the bar.

The William Howard Taft birthplace is a two-story brick home bought in 1851 by Alphonso Taft, who had it extensively remodeled to accomodate a growing family. The home remained in the family until 1899. In 1961, the Taft Memorial Association, under the leadership of Charles Phelps Taft II, son of the President, acquired control of the house and grounds. It was designated as a National Historic Site on December 2, 1969. The home and grounds have been restored by the National Park Service.
Location:
2038 Auburn Avenue, Cincinnati, Ohio.

**• WILLIAM HOWARD TAFT'S BIRTHPLACE
CINCINNATI, OHIO**

**WILLIAM HOWARD TAFT'S BURIAL SITE
ARLINGTON NATIONAL CEMETERY
ARLINGTON, VIRGINIA**

In 1921, President Warren Harding fulfilled Taft's long-cherished ambition by designating him as Chief Justice of the Supreme Court (1921-1930), in which position he served industriously and expedited the flow of court business.

Taft performed more than his share of the court's great work load, and frequently served as an adviser to President Calvin Coolidge. He watched his health carefully, and held his weight to about 300 pounds. The Chief Justice became a familiar figure in Washington, D.C. as he walked the three miles between his home and the court almost every morning and evening. But finally the strain of overwork became to great. Bad health, chiefly due to heart trouble, forced his retirement on February 3, 1930. Taft died on March 8, 1930 and was buried in Arlington National Cemetery.

Grave of William Howard Taft — 27th President of the United States 1909 - 1913. Chief Justice of the United States (1921 - 1930).

Location:

Entrance gate Memorial Drive off Jefferson Davis Highway. Arlington National Cemetery, Virginia.

■ **WILLIAM HOWARD TAFT'S BURIAL SITE
ARLINGTON NATIONAL CEMETERY
ARLINGTON, VIRGINIA**

WOODROW WILSON
28th President

Term — March 4, 1913
to March 4, 1921

Democratic Party

Birth: Staunton, Virginia. December 28, 1856

Zodiac Sign: Capricorn

Ancestry: Scotch - Irish

Father: Joseph Ruggles Wilson. Born: Steubenville, Ohio, February 28, 1822. Died: Princeton, New Jersey, January 21, 1903.

Mother: Jessie Janet Woodrow Wilson. Born: Carlisle, England, December 20, 1830. Died: Clarksville, Tennessee, April 15, 1888.

Sisters: Marion (1850 - 1890). Annie Josephine (1854 - 1916).

Brother: Joseph (1866 - ?).

First Wife: Ellen Louise Axson. Born: Savannah, Georgia, May 15, 1860. Died: Washington, D.C. (White House), August 6, 1914. Buried: Myrtle Hill, Rome, Georgia.

First Marraige: Savannah, Georgia. June 24, 1885.

Children: Margaret Woodrow (1886 - 1944). Jessie Woodrow (1887 - 1932). Eleanor Randolph (1889 - 1967).

Second Wife: Edith Bolling Galt. Born: Wytherville, Virginia, October 15, 1872. Died: Washington, D.C., December 28, 1961. Buried: Washington Cathedral, D.C. 1 crypt below her husband.

Second Marriage: Washington, D.C. December 18, 1915.

Education: Private tutors; Davidson College; Princeton University; University of Virginia Law School; John Hopkins University.

Religion: Presbyterian

Home: Woodrow Wilson House, 2340 South Street N.W., Washington, D.C.

Occupation Before Presidency: Lawyer; teacher; college president.

Pre-Presidential Offices: Governor of New Jersey.

Age at Inauguration: 56

Political Party: Democratic

Election of 1912

Candidates	Electoral Vote
Woodrow Wilson (Democratic)	435
Theodore Roosevelt (Progressive)	88
William H. Taft (Republican)	8
Eugene V. Debs (Socialist)	—
Eugene W. Chafin (Prohibition)	—

First Administration

President: Woodrow Wilson

Vice President: Thomas R. Marshall of Indiana

Inauguration: March 4, 1913

Election of 1916

Candidates	Electoral Vote
Woodrow Wilson (Democratic)	277
Charles E. Hughes (Republican)	254
A. L. Benson (Socialist)	—
J. Frank Hanly (Prohibition)	—

Second Administration

President: Woodrow Wilson

Vice President: Thomas R. Marshall of Indiana

Inauguration: March 5, 1917

The Capitol, Washington, D.C.

President at Time of Death: Calvin Coolidge

Death: Washington, D.C. February 3, 1924.

Cause of Death: Apoplexy at age 67.

Place of Burial: Washington Cathedral, Washington, D.C. Tomb of Woodrow Wilson inside cathedral.

"There must be, not a balance of power, but a community of power; not organized rivalries, but an organized common peace."

— Address to the Senate, 1917

WOODROW WILSON'S BIRTHPLACE
"THE MANSE", STAUNTON, VIRGINIA

WOODROW WILSON'S HOME
PRINCETON, NEW JERSEY

Thomas Woodrow Wilson, 28th President of the United States, was born in the simple, handsome "Manse" of the First Presbyterian Church in Staunton, Virginia on December 28, 1856.

Wilson was a thin, high-strung child who had to wear glasses. His mother called him a mischievous bundle of nerves.

The remarkable career of Woodrow Wilson, the son of a Presbyterian minister, reflects the enduring influence of a Christian family life. He served the nation and the world as an educator, statesman, president and architect of a reasoned plan for world peace.

A Registered National Historic Landmark, the Woodrow Wilson Birthplace is one of few Presidential birthplaces on view in its original form.

Location:

24 North Coalter Street on U.S. 11, Staunton, Virginia.

WOODROW WILSON'S HOME
PRINCETON, NEW JERSEY

Woodrow Wilson became professor of jurisprudence and political economy at the College of New Jersey in 1890 (Princeton University after 1896). As president of Princeton, from 1902 to 1910, Wilson won national fame as an educational reformer.

Woodrow Wilson resided in these two homes during his years at Princeton University.

Privately owned. Not open to the public.

Location:

72 Library Place. 82 Library Place. Princeton, New Jersey.

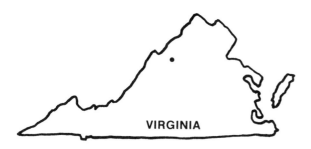

VIRGINIA

• WOODROW WILSON'S BIRTHPLACE
"THE MANSE", STAUNTON, VIRGINIA

**WOODROW WILSON'S HOUSE
WASHINGTON, D.C.**

When President Wilson left the White House in 1921, he retired with his wife to this townhouse. The Georgian-style townhouse is filled with Wilson memorabilia — from his books, typewriter, and clothes to World War I souvenirs and the only baseball autographed by a King (King George V). Unlike many other historic sites, the Woodrow Wilson house has the feeling of a comfortable home. Many of the rooms are filled with growing plants. (Mrs. Wilson liked plants.) On the second floor, inside an old Victrola, is a tape of Presidential favorites, including a Caruso rendition of "Johnny Get Your Gun". In the President's bedroom hangs a portrait of actress Jane Russell's mother. He bought it because of its resemblance to his first wife.

Woodrow Wilson lived in quiet retirement in Washington, D.C. after his presidential term ended in March 1921. He formed a law partnership with Bainbridge Colby, his third Secretary of State. Although Wilson had regained partial use of his arms and legs, his physical condition did not permit any actual work. He saw an occasional motion picture or play, listened to books and magazines read aloud to him, and sometimes invited friends for lunch.

After the President's death in 1924, Mrs. Wilson continued to live here for nearly forty years. Open as a historic house museum, Wilson House also serves as a community preservation center.

Location:

2340 S Street N.W., Near Dumont Circle, Washington D.C.

**WOODROW WILSON'S HOUSE
WASHINGTON, D.C.**

WOODROW WILSON'S BURIAL SITE
WASHINGTON NATIONAL CATHEDRAL
WASHINGTON, D.C.

On February 3, 1924, Woodrow Wilson died in his sleep. Two days later, Wilson was buried in the National Cathedral.

The Washington National Cathedral is a Gothic style edifice that, when completed, will be one of the largest cathedrals in the world. The center tower is the highest point in the District of Columbia.

Location:

Wisconsin and Massachusetts Avenue N.W., Washington, D.C.

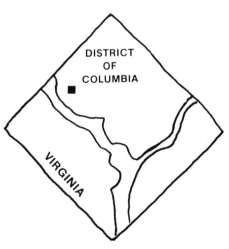

■ **WOODROW WILSON'S BURIAL SITE**
WASHINGTON NATIONAL CATHEDRAL
WASHINGTON, D.C.

WARREN G. HARDING
29th President

Term — March 4, 1921
to August 2, 1923

Republican Party

Birth: Bloomington Grove (Corsica), Ohio, November 2, 1865.

Zodiac Sign: Scorpio

Ancestry: English and Scotch - Irish

Father: George Tryon Harding. Born: Blooming Grove, Ohio, June 12, 1843. Died: Santa Ana, California, November 19, 1928.

Mother: Phoebe Elizabeth Dickerson. Born: Blooming Grove, Ohio, December 21, 1843. Died: May 20, 1910.

Brothers: Charles Alexander (1874 - 1878). George Tryon (1878 - 1934).

Sisters: Charity Malvina (1867 - 1951). Mary Clarissa (1868 - 1913). Eleanor Priscilla (1872 - 1878). Abigail Victoria (1875 - 1935). Phoebe Caroline (1879 - 1951).

Wife: Florence Kling De Wolfe. Born: Marion, Ohio, August 15, 1860. Died: Marion, Ohio, November 21, 1924. Buried: Harding Memorial, Marion, Ohio.

Marriage: Marion, Ohio. July 8, 1891.

Education: Local schools; Ohio Central College.

Religion: Baptist

Occupation Before Presidency: Newspaper editor

Pre-Presidential Offices: Member of the Ohio Senate; Lieutenant Governor of Ohio; U.S. Senator.

Political Party: Republican

Age at Inauguration: 55

Election of 1920

Candidates	Electoral Vote
Warren G. Harding (Republican)	404
James M. Cox (Democratic)	127
Eugene V. Debs (Socialist)	—
P. P. Christensen (Farmer Labor)	—
Aaron S. Watkins (Prohibition)	—

The Harding Administration
President: Warren G. Harding
Vice President: Calvin Coolidge of Massachusetts
Inauguration: March 4, 1921
The Capitol, Washington, D.C.

Death: San Francisco, California. August 2, 1923.

Cause of Death: Apoplexy at age 57.

Place of Burial: Harding Memorial, Marion, Ohio.

"We mean to have less of Government in business and more business in Government."
— Address to Congress, 1921

**WARREN G. HARDING'S BIRTHPLACE
BLOOMING GROVE, OHIO**

Warren G. Harding was born on November 2, 1865, on a farm near Corsica (now Blooming Grove), Ohio. He was the eldest of the eight children of George Tryon Harding and Pheobe Dickerson Harding. Warren attended grammer schools in Corsica and Caledonia. At the age of 14, he entered Ohio Central College at Iberia, and was graduated three years later.

The large historical marker designates the area and the small stone marker rests on the southwest corner of the actual location of the salt box cottage. The Harding farmhouse was built in 1856 and torn down in 1896.

Location:

Hwy. 97 and 288, Blooming Grove, Ohio.

**WARREN G. HARDING'S HOME
MARION, OHIO**

Warren Harding and Florence Kling De Wolfe designed the home and arranged for its construction in anticipation of their marriage, which took place in the large front hallway of the completed structure in July 1891. From the front porch of this home, Harding, then a United States Senator, conducted his famous "front porch campaign" in 1920. It was the Harding home from July 8, 1891, until they left for the White House on March 2, 1921, never to return. In accordance with the terms on Item 3 of the Will of Mrs. Harding, it was bequeathed in 1924 to the newly formed Harding Memorial Association to be "forever preserved".

During the winter of 1964-1965, the Harding Memorial Association restored the house to its appearance at the turn of the century. The original gas lights, wired for electricity, were put back in place; decorations especially the wallpaper, were duplicated in authentic detail; and the original furniture and furnishings were returned to their positions in the home.

Location:

380 Mount Vernon Avenue, Marion, Ohio.

OHIO

**• WARREN G. HARDING'S BIRTHPLACE
BLOOMING GROVE, OHIO**

**WARREN G. HARDING'S BURIAL SITE
HARDING MEMORIAL, MARION, OHIO**

In June 1923, President and Mrs. Harding began a trip across the continent and to Alaska, which ended with his death in San Francisco on August 2. The news brought deep sorrow to the nation. Following services in Washington, D.C., a funeral train carried the President's body to Marion, Ohio, where it was placed in a temporary tomb at Marion Cemetery. Later on December 21, 1927, the bodies of the President and Mrs. Harding, who died in Marion in 1924, were moved from the temporary tomb to the newly constructed Harding Memorial.

The Harding Memorial is a circular monument of white Georgia marble which contains the stone coffins of President Warren G. Harding and his wife, Florence Kling Harding. The monument is situated in the middle of ten acres of beautifully landscaped grounds, whose rows of maple trees form the shape of a Latin cross. The graves are covered by two slabs of emerald pearl Labrador granite. President Harding occupies the tomb marked by a bronze palm wreath, while Mrs. Harding occupies the tomb marked by a bronze wreath of roses.

Location:

Vernon Heights Blvd., Marion, Ohio.

**WARREN G. HARDING'S BURIAL SITE
HARDING MEMORIAL, MARION, OHIO**

OHIO

**■ WARREN G. HARDING'S BURIAL SITE
HARDING MEMORIAL, MARION, OHIO**

CALVIN COOLIDGE
30th President

Term — August 3, 1923
to March 4, 1929

Republican Party

Birth: Plymouth Notch, Vermont. July 4, 1872.
Zodiac Sign: Cancer
Ancestry: Ehglish
Father: John Calvin Coolidge. Born: Plymouth, Vermont, March 31, 1845. Died: Plymouth Notch, Vermont, March 18, 1926.
Mother: Victoria Josephine Moor Coolidge. Born: Pinney Hollow, Vermont, March 14, 1846. Died: Plymouth Notch, Vermont, March 14, 1885.
Sister: Abigail (1875 - 1890).
Wife: Grace Anna Goodhue. Born: Burlington, Vermont, January 3, 1879. Died: Northampton, Massachusetts, July 8, 1957. Buried: Plymouth Notch Cemetery, Plymouth, Vermont.
Marriage: Burlington, Vermont. October 4, 1905.
Children: John (1906 -   ). Calvin (1908 - 1924).
Education: Plymouth District school; Black River Academy; St. Johnsbury Academy; Amherst College.
Religion: Congregationalist
Home: Coolidge Homestead, Plymouth Notch, Vermont.
Occupation Before Presidency: Lawyer
Pre-Presidential Offices: Member of the Massachusetts House of Representatives; Mayor of Northampton, Massachusetts; Member and President of Massachusetts Senate; Lt. Governor of Massachusetts; Governor of Massachusetts; Vice President of the U.S.
Political Party: Republican
Age at Inauguration: 51
Note: The sixth Vice President who succeeded to the Presidency because of the death of his predecesor, Warren Harding.
First Administration
President: Calvin Coolidge
Inauguration: August 3, 1923
Plymouth Notch, Vermont

Election of 1924

Candidates	Electoral Vote
Calvin Coolidge (Republican)	382
John W. Davis (Democratic)	136
Robert M. LaFollette (Progressive)	13

Second Administration
President: Calvin Coolidge
Vice President: Charles G. Dawes of Illinois
Inauguration: March 4, 1925
Inauguration: March 4, 1925
The Capitol, Washington, D.C.
Occupation After Presidency: Writer
President at Time of Death: Herbert C. Hoover
Death: Northampton, Massachusetts. January 5, 1933.
Cause of Death: Coronary thrombosis at age 60.
Place of Burial: Plymouth Notch Cemetery, Plymouth, Vermont.

"Economy is idealism in its most practical form."
— Inaugural Address, 1925

**CALVIN COOLIDGE'S BIRTHPLACE
PLYMOUTH, VERMONT**

Calvin Coolidge was born on Independence Day, July 4, 1872, in Plymouth Notch, a village near Woodstock in central Vermont. He was named for his father, John Calvin Coolidge, but his parents called him Calvin, or Cal. He dropped the name John after leaving college.

Coolidge's mother, Victoria Josephine Moor Coolidge, died when he was 12 years old. The next year he entered Black River Academy at nearby Ludlow. He was graduated in 1890. He took a short course at St. Johnsbury Academy and entered Amherst College in 1891. He was graduated in 1895. Coolidge then read law with the firm of Hammond and Field in Northampton, Massachusetts. He passed the Massachusetts bar in 1897.

This building has been restored to the condition it was on July 4, 1872 when the President was born in the lower bedroom.

In 1968, the State of Vermont acquired the birthplace. With old photos as a guide, the exterior of the birthplace has been restored. The interior of the building when acquired by the State, was used as a private home and had been completely modernized.

After detailed studies of the original construction and with the invaluable aid of the former owners, the interior has been restored to its appearance in 1872. The birthplace is furnished with original artifacts from the Coolidge family.

Location:

On Vermont 100 A., Plymouth, Vermont.

VERMONT

• CALVIN COOLIDGE'S BIRTHPLACE
PLYMOUTH, VERMONT

CALVIN COOLIDGE'S BURIAL SITE
PLYMOUTH NOTCH CEMETERY
PLYMOUTH, VERMONT

South of Plymouth apiece lies the Plymouth Notch Cemetery where in the winter of 1933, President Coolidge was laid to rest alongside his son, Calvin, Jr., and generations of his family. Here also now lies his beloved wife, Grace Goodhue Coolidge, who died on July 8, 1957. The simple serenity of the village and surrounding mountains is appropriately reflected in the plain Vermont granite headstone that marks the President's grave.

Location:

About 1 mile southwest of Plymouth, Vermont on the south side of Vermont 100A. A country road leads to the cemetery. Plymouth, Vermont.

CALVIN COOLIDGE'S HOMESTEAD
PLYMOUTH, VERMONT

This Vermont homestead was, in 1923, the setting for the ceremony that made Mr. Coolidge the 30th President. Here as Vice President, Mr. Coolidge was vacationing when word came of the death of President Harding. In the bay-window room on the first floor, at 2:47 in the morning of August 3rd, Col. John Coolidge, a notary public, administered by the light of a kerosine lamp the oath as President of the United States to his son.

In later years, an inquisitive visitor asked Colonel Coolidge, "How did you know you could administer the Presidential oath to your son?" The laconic Vermonter replied, "I didn't know that I couldn't".

With the passage of years, the night-time drama enacted in this Vermont village home, becomes not only a firmer segment of our history, but continues to draw visitors from all over the world to Plymouth. In 1957, the President's son, John Coolidge and his wife Florence, gave to the Vermont Board of Historic Sites this original house complete with all the furnishings that were there on the night of the inauguration.

Location:

On Vermont 100 A, Plymouth, Vermont.

■ CALVIN COOLIDGE'S BURIAL SITE
PLYMOUTH NOTCH CEMETERY
PLYMOUTH, VERMONT

HERBERT HOOVER
31st President

Term — March 4, 1929 to March 4, 1933

Republican Party

Birth: West Branch, Iowa. August 10, 1874.
Zodiac Sign: Leo
Ancestry: Swiss - German
Father: Jesse Clark Hoover. Born: Miami County, Ohio, September 2, 1846. Died: West Branch, Iowa, December 14, 1880.
Mother: Hulda Randall Minthorn Hoover. Born: Burgerville, Ontario, Canada, May 4, 1849. Died: West Branch, Iowa, February 24, 1883.
Brother: Theodore Jesse Hoover (1871 - 1955).
Sister: Mary (May) Hoover (1876 - 1950).
Wife: Lou Henry. Born: Waterloo, Iowa, March 29, 1875. Died: New York, New York, January 7, 1944. Buried: West Branch, Iowa.
Marriage: Monterey, California. February 10, 1899.
Children: Herbert Clark (1903 - 1969). Allan Henry (1907 -).
Education: Local schools; Newberg Academy; graduated from Stanford University (1895).
Religion: Quaker
Home: Herbert Hoover Birthplace, West Branch, Iowa.
Occupation Before Presidency: Engineer
Pre-Presidential Offices: Chairman of Commission for Relief in Belgium; U.S. Food Administrator; Chairman of Supreme Economic Council; Secretary of Commerce.
Political Party: Republican
Age at Inauguration: 54
Election of 1928

Candidates	Electoral Vote
Herbert C. Hoover (Republican)	444
Alfred E. Smith (Democratic)	87
Norman Thomas (Socialist)	—

The Hoover Administration
President: Herbert C. Hoover
Vice President: Charles Curtis of Kansas. Son of an Abolitionist father and a Kaw Indian mother.
Inauguration: March 4, 1929
The Capitol, Washington, D.C.

Occupation After Presidency: Chairman of Commission for Polish Relief Fund; Chairman of Finnish Relief Fund; Coordinator of Food Supply for World Famine; Chairman of Commissions on Organization of the Executive Branch of the Government (Hoover Commissions); writer.
President at Time of Death: Lyndon B. Johnson
Death: New York, New York. October 20, 1964.
Cause of Death: Internal hemorrhage at age 90.
Place of Burial: Hoover Presidential Library, West Branch, Iowa.

"The greatness of America has grown out of a political and social system and a method of control of economic forces distinctly its own — our American system . . ."
— Rugged Individualism, 1928

HERBERT HOOVER'S BIRTHPLACE
WEST BRANCH, IOWA

HERBERT HOOVER
QUAKER MEETINGHOUSE
WEST BRANCH, IOWA

Herbert Hoover was the first President born west of the Mississippi River. He was born in West Branch, Iowa, on August 10, 1874. One of his ancestors, Andrew Huber (Hoover), had come to Pennsylvania from Germany in 1738. Huber, a Quaker, moved to North Carolina. His descendants settled in Ohio, and moved to Iowa in 1853.

Hoover's father died of typhoid fever in 1880. Huldah Hoover, Herbert's mother, supported the family by preaching and sewing. She died of pneumonia when Herbert was eight years old, and relatives reared the children.

In 1885, Hoover went to Newberg, Oregon to live with his uncle, Henry J. Minthorn. Hoover received his secondary school at Newberg College. In 1890, Hoover became interested in engineering and enrolled in the first class of the newly founded Stanford University in Palo Alto, California, and graduated in 1895.

Built by Jesse Clark Hoover in 1871, the little two-room birthplace cottage, now restored and refurnished, stands on its original site. The Hoovers lived in the house until 1879, when Jesse Hoover sold both it and the blacksmith shop and moved his family into a larger dwelling farther south on Downey Street. When the birthplace cottage was restored to its 1871 appearance in 1939, as much as possible of the original furniture belonging to Jesse and Hulda Hoover was acquired for the house.

Location:
10 miles east of Iowa City, Iowa off Interstate 80. West Branch, Iowa.

During his years in West Branch, Herbert Hoover attended meetings here with his parents. In fact, his mother often spoke before the congregation that worshipped in the building. Neglected for many years, the meetinghouse was purchased by the people of West Branch in 1964 and presented to the Herbert Hoover Birthplace Foundation. In 1964-1965, after being moved to its present location on the east side of Downey Street opposite the Presidential Library and southeast of the birthplace cottage, the meetinghouse was restored to its near original appearance.

Location:
10 miles east of Iowa City, Iowa off Interstate 80. West Branch, Iowa.

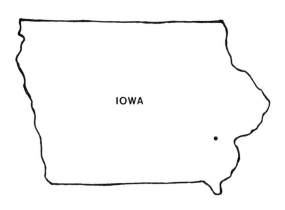

IOWA

• HERBERT HOOVER'S BIRTHPLACE
WEST BRANCH, IOWA

**HERBERT HOOVER'S BOYHOOD HOME
"MINTHORN HOUSE", NEWBERG, OREGON**

**GEORGE FOX COLLEGE
NEWBERG, OREGON**

Minthorn House, the boyhood home of Herbert Hoover, Newberg, Oregon. At the age of ten, Hoover came to live with his uncle, Dr. Henry John Minthorn. Like Hoover's parents, Minthorn was a Quaker. He had lost his own son and was eager to provide a warm home for the orphaned Herbert.

Location:

One block south of Highway 99W on River Street, Newberg, Oregon.

**GEORGE FOX COLLEGE
NEWBERG, OREGON**

Herbert Hoover received his secondary school education at Newberg College, now George Fox College, a small Quaker academy in Newberg, Oregon. His uncle was principal of the academy. The boy attended the school from the time he was 11 until he was 15.

Location:

George Fox College, Newberg, Oregon.

HERBERT HOOVER'S BURIAL SITE
WEST BRANCH, IOWA

Herbert Hoover died in his suite at the Waldorf-Astoria Hotel in New York City October 20, 1964, and his flag draped coffin was carried with full military honors to Washington, D.C., to lie in state in the Capitol Rotunda. On October 25, 80,000 people assembled in West Branch to observe the burial ceremony.

On a hillside about ¼ mile southwest of the birthplace cottage are the graves of President and Mrs. Hoover. Landscaping provides a circular setting for the flat, white marble gravestones, and a vista to the birthplace cottage.

Location:

10 miles east of Iowa City, Iowa off Interstate 80. West Branch, Iowa.

HERBERT HOOVER PRESIDENTIAL LIBRARY AND MUSEUM
WEST BRANCH, IOWA

The library-museum houses the large collection of papers accumulated by Hoover during his many years of public service. It also holds his collection of books and objects associated with his long, distinguished career. Many items are on display in exhibit areas. A 180 seat auditorium occupies one wing of the building. The library-museum was built by the Hoover Birthplace Foundation. The gift of the buildings and grounds by the foundation to the Nation was accepted August 10, 1964.

Location:

10 miles east of Iowa City, Iowa off Interstate 80. West Branch, Iowa.

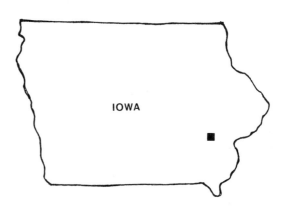

■ HERBERT HOOVER'S BURIAL SITE
WEST BRANCH, IOWA

119

FRANKLIN D. ROOSEVELT
32nd President

Term — March 4, 1933 to April 12, 1945

Democratic Party

Birth: Hyde Park, New York. January 30, 1882.

Zodiac Sign: Aquarius

Ancestry: Dutch

Father: James Roosevelt. Born: Hyde Park, New York, July 16, 1828. Died: New York, New York, December 8, 1900.

Mother: Sara Delano Roosevelt. Born: Newburgh, New York, September 21, 1854. Died: Hyde Park, New York, September 7, 1941.

Half Brother: James Roosevelt (1854 - 1927).

Wife: Anna Eleanor Roosevelt. Born: New York, New York, October 11, 1884. Died: New York, New York, November 7, 1962. Buried: Hyde Park, New York.

Marriage: New York, New York. March 17, 1905.

Children: Anna Eleanor (1906 - 1975). James (1907 -). Franklin (1909 - 1909). Elliott (1910 -). second Franklin Delano Jr. (1914 -). John Aspinwall (1916 - 1981).

Education: Private tutor; Groton School; B.A. from Harvard University (1903); studied law at Columbia University.

Religion: Episcopalian

Home: Hyde Park, New York

Occupation Before Presidency: Lawyer; politician.

Pre-Presidential Offices: Member of New York State Senate; Assistant Secretary of the Navy; Governor of New York.

Political Party: Democratic

Age at Inauguration: 51

Election of 1932

Candidates	Electoral Vote
Franklin D. Roosevelt (Democratic)	472
Herbert C. Hoover (Republican)	59
Norman Thomas (Socialist)	—
William Z. Foster (Communist)	—
William D. Upshaw (Prohibition)	—

First Administration

President: Franklin D. Roosevelt
Vice President: John N. Garner of Texas
Inauguration: March 4, 1933
The Capitol, Washington, D.C.

Election of 1936

Candidates	Electoral Vote
Franklin D. Roosevelt (Democratic)	523
Alfred M. Landon (Republican)	8
William Lemke (Union)	—
Norman Thomas (Socialist)	—
Earl Browder (Communist)	—

Second Administration

President: Franklin D. Roosevelt
Vice President: John N. Garner of Texas
Inauguration: January 20, 1937
The Capitol, Washington, D.C.

Election of 1940

Candidates	Electoral Vote
Franklin D. Roosevelt (Democratic)	449
Wendell L. Willkie (Republican)	82
Norman Thomas (Socialist)	—

Third Administration

President: Franklin D. Roosevelt
Vice President: Henry A. Wallace of Iowa
Inauguration: January 20, 1941
The Capitol, Washington, D.C.

Election of 1944

Candidates	Electoral Vote
Franklin D. Roosevelt (Democratic)	432
Thomas E. Dewey (Republican)	99
Norman Thomas (Socialist)	—

Fourth Administration

President: Franklin Roosevelt
Vice President: Harry S. Truman of Missouri
Inauguration: January 20, 1945
The White House, Washington, D.C.

Death: Warm Springs, Georgia. April 12, 1945.

Cause of Death: Cerebral hemorrhage at age 63.

Place of Burial: Hyde Park, New York.

"The world order which we seek is the co-operation of free countries, working together in a friendly, civilized society."

— Four Freedoms Address, 1941

**FRANKLIN D. ROOSEVELT'S BIRTHPLACE
HYDE PARK, NEW YORK**

**FRANKLIN D. ROOSEVELT'S LITTLE WHITE HOUSE
WARM SPRINGS, GEORGIA**

Franklin Delano Roosevelt was born January 30, 1882, on his father's estate, "Springwood", in Hyde Park, N.Y. He was the only child of James and Sara Roosevelt. James Roosevelt was a wealthy Vice President of the Delaware and Hudson Railway. His wife was a member of the wealthy Delano family. When Franklin was born, his mother was 28 years old and his father was 54.

From the time he was 3 years old, Franklins parents usually took him on their yearly trips to Europe. He studied under governesses and private tutors until he was 14. He learned to speak and write both German & French. At the age of 14, Roosevelt entered Groton School, a preparatory school in Groton, Massachusetts. He was graduated from Groton in 1900.

Roosevelt enrolled that same year at Harvard University, and was graduated from Harvard in 1903. In 1904 he entered the Columbia University Law School.

Location:

1 mile south of Hyde Park on US 9 (Albany Post Road) Hyde Park, New York.

NEW YORK

● **FRANKLIN D. ROOSEVELT'S BIRTHPLACE
HYDE PARK, NEW YORK**

The "Little White House", located on a beautiful site on the slopes of Pine Mountain, tells much of the nature of the man who played such an important role in the history of this country and of the world. It is an impressive home, but is small, with comfort and utility stressed. Original plans were altered by Mr. Roosevelt to remove features he considered to elaborate, and the Little White House, with three bedrooms, has only an entry, a combination living and dining room, a kitchen, and a spacious sun deck.

During his entire time in office, Mr. Roosevelt used the Little White House frequently. He had come to Warm Springs first in 1924 to test its pools as an aid in recovery from infantile paralysis which struck him in 1921. Finding exercise in the warm bouyant water beneficial, he became interested in developing the resort for others similarly afflicted, so the Georgia Warm Springs Foundation and subsequent development of health facilities resulted from his own efforts.

Retained substantially as it was when he died there April 12, 1945, the Little White House still holds the personality Mr. Roosevelt gave it. A lone wheel chair is a reminder of his affliction. But keys to his personality are many, numerous ship models are located in the home of the man who had such a great love of the sea. Fala's dog chain, and a riding quirt still hang in the closet. Mememtos which he cherished more because of the givers than for the workmanship, are on the walls, some the products of school children.

Location:

On U.S. 27A and Georgia 85W. Warm Springs, Georgia.

**FRANKLIN D. ROOSEVELT'S BURIAL SITE
HYDE PARK, NEW YORK**

Franklin D. Roosevelt died April 12, 1945, at his "Little White House" at Warm Springs, Georgia.

April 12 began as usual. The President read newspapers and mail that had been flown from Washington, D.C.

Roosevelt was working at his desk while an artist, Mrs. Elizabeth Schoumatoff, painted his portrait. Suddenly he fell over in his chair. "I have a terrific headache", he whispered. These were Roosevelt's last words. He died a few hours later of a cerebral hemorrhage.

As news of his death spread, a crowd gathered in front of the White House, silent with grief. Millions of people in all parts of the world mourned the dead President.

Roosevelt was buried in the rose garden at Hyde Park, New York.

Location:

One mile south of Hyde Park on U.S. 9 (Albany Post Road), Hyde Park, New York.

**■ FRANKLIN D. ROOSEVELT'S BURIAL SITE
HYDE PARK, NEW YORK**

**FRANKLIN D. ROOSEVELT LIBRARY AND MUSEUM
HYDE PARK, NEW YORK**

The Franklin D. Roosevelt Library was established as part of the National Archives by joint resolution of the Congress in 1939. Erected and equipped by a private foundation on 16 acres of the President's Hyde Park estate, the building and grounds were turned over to the government on July 4, 1940.

The research collections are made up of manuscripts and other documents, the most important of which are the papers bequeathed to the American people by Franklin D. Roosevelt. They reflect his entire life, as well as an important part of the history of our time. Eleanor Roosevelt's papers are also housed in the library.

The museum, open to the public, contains extensive displays on the life and career of F.D.R., including photographs, objects that he used personally or received as gifts; selected items from his collection on the U.S. Navy, and many of his family letters, speeches, state documents, and official correspondence.

On May 3, 1972, two wings to the original building were dedicated in honor of Eleanor Roosevelt. One wing contains enlarged research facilities, the other contains an exhibition gallery devoted to Mrs. Roosevelt's life and career.

Location:

One mile south of Hyde Park on U.S. 9 (Albany Post Road), Hyde Park, New York.

HARRY S. TRUMAN
33rd President

Term — April 12, 1945
to January 20, 1953

Democratic Party

Birth: Lamar, Missouri. May 8, 1884

Zodiac Sign: Taurus

Ancestry: Scotch - Irish - English

Father: John Anderson Truman. Born: Jackson County, Missouri, December 5, 1851. Died: Grandview, Missouri, November 3, 1914.

Mother: Martha Ellen Young Truman. Born: Jackson County, Missouri, November 25, 1852. Died: Grandview, Missouri, July 26, 1947.

Brother: J. Vivian (1886 - 1965).

Sister: Mary Jane (1889 - 1978).

Wife: Elizabeth Virginia Wallace. Born: Independence, Missouri, February 13, 1885. Died: Independence, Missouri, October 18, 1982.

Marriage: Independence, Missouri. June 28, 1919.

Children: Margaret (1924 -   ).

Education: Graduated from public high school.

Religion: Baptist

Occupation Before Presidency: Railroad timekeeper; bank clerk; farmer; haberdasher.

Military Service: Missouri National Guard; Captain in 129th Field Artillery (1918 - 1919).

Pre-Presidential Offices: County Judge for Eastern District of Jackson County, Missouri; Presiding Judge, County Court, Jackson County, Missouri; United States Senator; Vice President of the U.S.

Age at Inauguration: 60

Note: The seventh Vice President who succeeded to the Presidency because of the death of his predecessor, Franklin D. Roosevelt.

First Administration
President: Harry S. Truman
Inauguration: April 12, 1945
The White House, Washington, D.C.

Election of 1948

Candidates	Electoral Vote
Harry S. Truman (Democratic)	303
Thomas E. Dewey (Republican)	189
Strom Thurmond (State's Rights)	39
Henry Wallace (Progressive)	—
Norman Thomas (Socialist)	—
Claude A. Watson (Prohibition)	—

Second Administration
President: Harry S. Truman
Vice President: Alben W. Barkley of Kentucky
Inauguration: January 20, 1949
The Capitol, Washington, D.C.

Occupation After Presidency: Writer

President at Time of Death: Richard M. Nixon

Death: Kansas City, Missouri. December 26, 1972.

Cause of Death: Debility at age 88.

Place of Burial: Harry S. Truman Library and Museum, Independence, Missouri.

"The responsibility of the great states is to serve and not to dominate the world."

— Address to Congress, 1945

**HARRY S. TRUMAN'S BIRTHPLACE
LAMAR, MISSOURI**

President Truman was born in the downstairs southwest bedroom, May 8, 1884. To give you an idea of how small the rooms are in the house, the bedroom where President Truman was born measured only 6 feet, 6 inches by 10 feet, 9 inches.

During the time the Truman family lived in Lamar, the father bought and sold livestock, primarily horses and mules.

President Truman was ten months old when the family moved to Harrisonville, Missouri.

The Truman birthplace was acquired by the United Automobile Workers and donated to the State of Missouri for the creation of a historic site.

The restoration of the house was governed in all aspects by a desire to recreate the atmosphere of the home at the time of President Truman's birth. It was dedicated on April 19, 1959.

Location:

1009 Truman Avenue, Lamar, Missouri.

**• HARRY S. TRUMAN'S BIRTHPLACE
LAMAR, MISSOURI**

HARRY S. TRUMAN'S BOYHOOD HOME
INDEPENDENCE, MISSOURI

HARRY S. TRUMAN'S HOME
"TRUMAN HOUSE", INDEPENDENCE, MISSOURI

The Truman House is an excellant example of mid-19th century Victorian architecture. The construction date is unknown, but George P. Gates, Bess Truman's maternal grandfather, purchased the lot in 1867. About 1903, after the death of her husband, Bess Truman's mother moved into her parent's residence. In 1924 she acquired full title to it. After her death in 1952, it became the property of the Truman's.

The home was the late president's residence from 1919. It served as the summer White House from 1945 to 1952.

Location:
    219 North Delaware Street, Independence, Missouri.

HARRY S. TRUMAN'S BOYHOOD HOME
INDEPENDENCE, MISSOURI

In 1895 John and Martha Truman bought this house, built about 1886. Harry S. Truman spent his boyhood here. The family moved in 1902. Later additions have greatly altered the original appearance of the house.

Location:
    909 West Waldo Street, Independence, Missouri.

Other boyhood homes:
    619 South Crysler Street and 902 North Liberty Street, Independence, Missouri.

    Privately owned. Not open to the public.

HARRY S. TRUMAN'S BURIAL SITE
HARRY S. TRUMAN LIBRARY AND MUSEUM
INDEPENDENCE, MISSOURI

Mr. Truman died December 26, 1972 at Kansas City, Missouri.

In his last days, Mr. Truman's tenaciousness impressed his doctors, one of whom said his fight against death "was a reflection of his attitude toward life". He was human and tough and fallible, and he will be sorely missed.

He is buried in the courtyard at the Harry S. Truman Library.

Location:

Delaware Street and U.S. 24, Independence, Missouri.

HARRY S. TRUMAN LIBRARY AND MUSEUM
INDEPENDENCE, MISSOURI

"This library will belong to the people of the United States. My papers will be the property of the people and be accessible to them. And this is as it should be. The papers of the President's are among the most valuable sources of material for history. They ought to be preserved and they ought to be used."
— Harry S. Truman

The library was built and furnished by the Harry S. Truman Library Inc., without cost to the government from funds donated by thousands of individuals and organizations in all parts of the country. It was dedicated July 6, 1957. Exhibits centered about the nature and history of the Presidency are an outstanding feature of the library.

Location:

U.S. 24 and Delaware Street, Independence, Missouri.

■ HARRY S. TRUMAN'S BURIAL SITE
HARRY S. TRUMAN LIBRARY AND MUSEUM
INDEPENDENCE, MISSOURI

DWIGHT D. EISENHOWER
34th President

**Term — January 20, 1953
to January 20, 1961**

Republican Party

Birth: Denison, Texas. October 14, 1890.

Zodiac Sign: Libra

Ancestry: Swiss - German

Father: David Jacob Eisenhower. Born: Elizabethville, Pennsylvania, September 23, 1863. Died: Abilene, Kansas, March 10, 1942.

Mother: Ida Elizabeth Stover Eisenhower. Born: Mount Sidney, Virginia, May 1, 1862. Died: Abilene, Kansas, September 11, 1946.

Brothers: Arthur (1886 - 1958). Edgar (1889 - 1971). Roy (1892 - 1942). Paul (1894 - 1894). Earl (1898 - 1968). Milton (1899-1985).

Wife: Mamie Geneva Doud. Born: Boone, Iowa, November 14, 1896. Died: Walter Reed Army Medical Center, Washington, D.C., November 1, 1979. Buried: Eisenhower Center, Abilene, Kansas.

Marriage: Denver, Colorado. July 1, 1916.

Children: Doud Dwight (1917 - 1921). John Sheldon (1922 -   ).

Education: Public schools; U.S. Military Academy, West Point, New York (graduated 1915).

Religion: Presbyterian

Military Service: Commissioned 2nd Lt. in U.S. Army (1915); served in various posts in United States, Panama, and Philippines (1915 - 1942); named Commander of European Theater of Operations (1942); named Supreme Commander of Allied Expeditionary Forces in Western Europe (1943); promoted to General of the Army (1944); named Army Chief of Staff (1945); Appointed Supreme Commander of Allied Powers of Europe (1951).

Age at Inauguration: 62

Election of 1952

Candidates	Electoral Vote
Dwight D. Eisenhower (Republican)	442
Adlai E. Stevenson (Democratic)	89
Vincent Hallinan (Progressive)	—

First Administration
President: Dwight D. Eisenhower
Vice President: Richard M. Nixon of California
Inauguration: January 20, 1953
The Capitol, Washington, D.C.

Election of 1956

Candidates	Electoral Vote
Dwight D. Eisenhower (Republican)	457
Adlai E. Stevenson (Democratic)	73
T. Coleman Andrews (States Rights)	—

Second Administration
President: Dwight D. Eisenhower
Vice President: Richard M. Nixon of California
Inauguration: January 20, 1957
The Capitol, Washington, D.C.

Occupation After Presidency: Writer; Retired General of the Army.

President at Time of Death: Richard M. Nixon

Death: Walter Reed Hospital, Washington, D.C. March 28, 1969.

Cause of Death: Heart attack at age 78.

Place of Burial: Meditation Chapel, Eisenhower Center, Abilene, Kansas.

"The quest for peace is the statesman's most exacting duty . . . Practical progress to lasting peace is his fondest hope."

— Geneva Conference Address, 1955

**DWIGHT D. EISENHOWER'S BIRTHPLACE
DENISON, TEXAS**

On October 14, 1890. Dwight D. Eisenhower, future five-star General of the Army and two-term President of the United States, was born in a modest two-story frame house in Denison, Texas. The Eisenhower family lived here for three years while the father, David, worked as an engine wiper with the Missouri, Kansas, and Texas Railroad, known as the Katy. The spring after Dwight's birth, his family moved to Abilene, Kansas. Eisenhower entered West Point Military Academy in 1911. He was graduated in 1915, 61st in a class of 164.

Recognition of the birthplace was late in coming. Even Eisenhower was unaware of the house, since he listed Tyler, Texas as his birthplace upon entering West Point. He was the only one of seven boys born to the Eisenhower's who was born in Texas. The rest of the children were born in Kansas.

Although a quilt in the bedroom where Ike was born is the only authentic Eisenhower possession in the house, the furnishings were chosen to be representative of the 1890's. The exterior has been restored, and a railed upstairs porch which had been part of the house when built circa 1880 was reconstructed.

Location:

208 East Day Street, Denison, Texas.

**DWIGHT D. EISENHOWER'S BIRTHPLACE
DENISON, TEXAS**

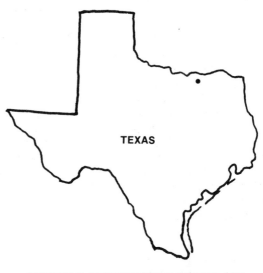

TEXAS

**• DWIGHT D. EISENHOWER'S BIRTHPLACE
DENISON, TEXAS**

128

DWIGHT D. EISENHOWER CENTER
EISENHOWER FAMILY HOME
ABILENE, KANSAS

A simple frame structure, typical of family homes in the Midwest in the late nineteenth century, the Eisenhower Family Home was occupied by members of the family from 1898 until 1946. After the death of General Eisenhower's mother, Mrs. Ida Elizabeth Eisenhower in 1946, it was given to the Eisenhower Foundation by her sons on the condition that it would be preserved without change and would be always open to the public without charge. The interior, with its family furniture and mementos arranged as they were at the time of Mrs. Eisenhower's death in 1946, is shown to visitors on escorted tours. The home was given to the United States by the Eisenhower Foundation in 1966.

Visitors from all over the world have been impressed by the simplicity of this National Shrine, the home of one of America's outstanding families. Since June 1947, the home has been open daily and thousands of people from all states, territories, and many foreign countries have registered as visitors.

Location:
201 S.E. 4th Street. East of Kansas Highway 15 and two miles south of Abilene exit from Interstate 70, Abilene, Kansas.

DWIGHT D. EISENHOWER CENTER
EISENHOWER LIBRARY
ABILENE, KANSAS

"When this library is filled with documents, and scholars come here to probe into some of the facts of the past half century, I hope that they, as we today, are concerned primarily with the ideals, principles, and trends that provide guides to a free, rich peaceful future in which all peoples can achieve ever-rising levels of human well-being. Those who have so generously made possible the construction of this library do not seek reward or acclaim. Yet, I profoundly believe that they feel deep gratification in the knowledge that thus they may have helped in some small measure to assure the Nation's eternal adherence to these simple ideals and principles as free men shape historic trends toward noble goals."

President Dwight D. Eisenhower at the ground-breaking ceremonies for the library, October 13, 1959.

Location:
201 S.E. 4th Street. East of Kansas Highway 15 and two miles south of Abilene exit from Interstate 70, Abilene, Kansas.

DWIGHT D. EISENHOWER'S BURIAL SITE
PLACE OF MEDITATION
ABILENE, KANSAS

This building is the final resting place of Dwight D. Eisenhower, his wife Mamie Doud Eisenhower, and their son, Doud Dwight Eisenhower. It was designed to harmonize with the museum and library. Outstanding elements of its interior design are the richly colored windows, the Travertine wall panels and the walnut woodwork.

Location:

201 S.E. 4th Street. East of Kansas Highway 15 and two miles south of Abilene exit from Interstate 70, Abilene, Kansas.

DWIGHT D. EISENHOWER'S RETIREMENT HOME
GETTYSBURG, PENNSYLVANIA

Near the edge of historic Gettysburg, stands the farm that Dwight D. Eisenhower purchased after his retirement from the U.S. Army. During his Presidential years, he used it as a retreat; later it became his main residence.

Except for the winters, which he spent in California, Eisenhower resided at the farm until his death in Washington's Walter Reed Hospital in March 1969.

Eisenhower National Historic Site comprises about 493 acres.

Location:

Adams County, adjacent to the southwest boundary of Gettysburg National Military Park, Gettysburg, Pennsylvania.

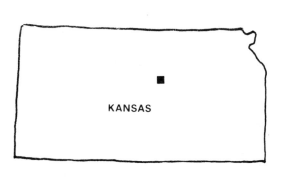

■ **DWIGHT D. EISENHOWER'S BURIAL SITE**
PLACE OF MEDITATION
ABILENE, KANSAS

JOHN F. KENNEDY
35th President

Term — January 20, 1961 to November 22, 1963

Democratic Party

Birth: Brookline, Massachusetts. May 29, 1917.

Zodiac Sign: Gemini

Ancestry: Irish

Father: Joseph P. Kennedy. Born: East Boston, Massachusetts, September 6, 1888. Died: Hyannis Port, Massachusetts, November 18, 1969.

Mother: Rose Fitzgerald Kennedy. Born: Boston, Massachusetts, July 22, 1890.

Brothers: Joseph Patrick (1915 - 1944). Robert Francis (1925 - 1968). Edward Moore (1932 -   ).

Sisters: Rosemary (1919 -   ). Kathleen (1920 - 1948). Eunice Mary (1921 -   ). Patricia (1924 -   ). Jean Ann (1928 -   ).

Wife: Jacqueline Lee Bouvier. Born: Southampton, New York, July 28, 1929.

Marriage: Newport, Rhode Island. September 12, 1953.

Children: Caroline Bouvier (1957 -   ). John Fitzgerald (1960 -   ). Patrick Bouvier (1963 - 1963).

Education: Attended the Choate School; London School of Economics; Princeton University; graduated from Harvard University (1940); Stanford University.

Religion: Roman Catholic

Occupation Before Presidency: Author

Military Service: Ensign, lieutenant (J.G.), lieutenant, U.S. Naval Reserve (active duty 1941 - 1945).

Pre-Presidential Offices: Member of the U.S. House of Representatives; Member U.S. Senate.

Age at Inauguration: 43

Election of 1960

Candidates	Electoral vote
John F. Kennedy (Democratic)	303
Richard M. Nixon (Republican)	219

The Kennedy Administration

President: John F. Kennedy
Vice President: Lyndon B. Johnson of Texas
Inauguration: January 20, 1961
The Capitol, Washington, D.C.

Death: Dallas, Texas. November 22, 1963.

Cause of Death: Assassination at age 46. November 22, 1963, shot by Lee Harvey Oswald, while in a motorcade in Dallas, Texas.

Place of Burial: Arlington National Cemetery, Arlington, Virginia.

"In the long history of the world, only a few generations have been granted the role of defending freedom in its hour of maximum danger . . . The energy, the faith, the devotion which we bring to this endeavor will light our country and all who serve it, and the glow from that fire can truly light the world."

— Inaugural Address, 1961

**JOHN FITZGERALD KENNEDY'S BIRTHPLACE
BROOKLINE, MASSACHUSETTS**

John Fitzgerald Kennedy, 35th President of the United States, was born and spent his babyhood in this house at 83 Beals Street in the Boston suburb of Brookline. In reminiscing about those days, his mother, Mrs. Joseph Kennedy, said that "every mother can influence her son to a great extent . . . And what you do with him and for him has influence, not for a day or for a year, but for time and eternity".

In this house John F. Kennedy learned the basic skills each man must learn: to walk, to talk, and laugh and pray.

In 1921, when he was four years old, the family moved having sold the house to the wife of Edward E. Moore, a close friend and business associate. Since then, the house has had various private owners. It was repurchased by the Kennedy family in 1966. Rose Kennedy has supervised the restoration and refurnishing of the house to its appearance in 1917.

The town of Brookline marked a commemorative plaque in 1961, and the house was designated a National Historic Landmark in May 1965. Two years later, Congress authorized its inclusion in the National Park System and made it a National Historic Site.

Location:

83 Beals Street, Brookline, Massachusetts.

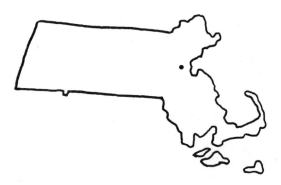

**• JOHN FITZGERALD KENNEDY'S BIRTHPLACE
BROOKLINE, MASSACHUSETTS**

JOHN F. KENNEDY'S SUMMER HOME
KENNEDY COMPOUND
HYANNIS PORT, MASSACHUSETTS

JOHN F. KENNEDY'S ASSASSINATION SITE
TEXAS SCHOOL BOOK DEPOSITORY
DALLAS, TEXAS

The Kennedy Compound consists of about six acres of waterfront property along Nantucket Sound. It contains the homes of Joseph P. Kennedy, and two of his sons, Robert F., and John F. During the late 1950's and early 1960's, the latter utilized the compound as a base for his Presidential campaign and as a summer White House and Presidential retreat until his assassination in 1963.

Location:

Irving and Marchant Avenues, Hyannis Port, Massachusetts.

Not open to the public.

John F. Kennedy was shot to death by an assassin on November 22, 1963, as he rode through the streets of Dallas, Texas.

Kennedy came to Texas accompanied by his wife and Vice President Johnson and Mrs. Lyndon B. Johnson. The chief purpose of his trip was to heal a split in the Texas Democratic party before the 1964 Presidential campaign in which Kennedy planned to run for his second term in office.

Plans called for the President, Mrs. Kennedy, Johnson and others to travel in a motorcade through the streets of Dallas to the Dallas Trade Mart.

The motorcade route took the Presidential car around a sharp left turn and down an incline toward a triple underpass. Loaming over the turn is an old seven-story brick building, a warehouse called the Texas School Book Depository.

Lee Harvey Oswald was standing at a sixth floor window tracking the presidential limousine through the telescopic sight of a rifle.

Mrs. John Connally, wife of Governor John Connally, turned smilingly to the President and said, "you can't say that Dallas isn't friendly to you today". Jack Kennedy's reply was cut off by the sharp brutal sound of a gunshot.

At the crack of the shot, the President jerked sharply and clutched his neck. As Kennedy slumped forward a third shot was fired.

The Presidential limousine roared away from the scene of the shooting to Parkland Hospital.

In the emergency room, one doctor worked feverishly over the President. Jackie Kennedy stood quietly by, looking "brave — but fear was in her eyes". She called for a priest. At 1:33 PM a press aide announced that the President of the United States was dead.

Location:

Houston and Elm Streets, Dallas, Texas.

JOHN F. KENNEDY'S ASSASSINATION SITE
TRIPLE UNDERPASS
DALLAS, TEXAS

**JOHN F. KENNEDY MEMORIAL PLAZA
ASSASSINATION SITE
DALLAS, TEXAS**

**JOHN FITZGERALD KENNEDY LIBRARY
COLUMBIA POINT, DORCHESTER, MASSACHUSETTS**

This library is an educational and research center dealing with the life and times of the 35th President of the United States and the American system of politics and government. In spirit and in fact it belongs to the people of the United States. Like all the Nation's Presidential Libraries, it is part of the National Archives of the Federal government. The building was built with funds donated by millions of people, young and old, and was given to the United States Government on October 20, 1979. The health of democracy in America depends upon informed citizens who understand the benefits and responsibilities of a free society and who are prepared to join in seeking new and better answers to the age old problems confronting humanity. We hope this library contributes to the fulfillment of that goal, and that it transmits to you some of John F. Kennedy's own enthusiasm and love for our American system of politics and government.

Location:

From the south: Rt. 3 to Dorchester, take Exit 18 to Morrissey Boulevard. Follow signs to J.F.K. Library.

From the west: Mass. Turnpike Rt. I-90 to Expressway Rt. 3/I-90, south bound to Exit 17, follow signs to J.F.K. Library.

From the north: Rt. I-93 or Rte. I-95 South to Boston, and on to S.E. Expressway Rts. 3/I-93. Take Exit 17, follow signs to J.F.K. Library. Dorchester, Massachusetts.

**JOHN F. KENNEDY MEMORIAL PLAZA
ASSASSINATION SITE
DALLAS, TEXAS**

This landscape city block with open style 30 ft. monument designed by Philip Johnson and dedicated to President Kennedy is situated 200 yards from the spot where President Kennedy was assassinated in Dallas, Texas.

Location:

Main, Commerce and Market Streets, Dallas, Texas.

**JOHN F. KENNEDY'S BURIAL SITE
ARLINGTON NATIONAL CEMETERY
ARLINGTON, VIRGINIA**

The sudden death of President Kennedy shocked the world. Many persons said that the assassination resulted from an atmosphere of hate and violence that had been created by extremist political groups.

Kennedy's body was brought back to the White House and placed in the East Room for 24 hours. On the Sunday after the assassination, the President's flag-draped coffin was carried to the Capitol rotunda to lie in state. Throughout the day and night, hundreds of thousands of persons filed past the guarded casket.

Kennedy was buried with full military honors at Arlington National Cemetery across the Potomac River from Washington on November 25, 1963. At the close of the funeral service, Mrs. Kennedy lighted an eternal flame to burn forever over the President's grave.

Construction of the permanent memorial and gravesite for the late President began in September 1965. The remains of President Kennedy and of two infants, a son and a daughter, who pre-deceased their father, were removed to the permanent gravesite during the evening of March 14, 1967. The gravesite was blessed by Richard Cardinal Cushing at brief ceremonies held the morning of March 15, 1967.

Location:

South Gate, Arlington National Cemetery, Arlington, Virginia.

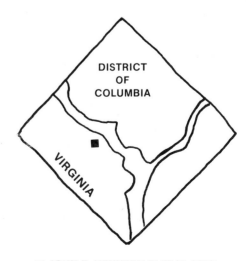

**■ JOHN F. KENNEDY BURIAL SITE
ARLINGTON NATIONAL CEMETERY
ARLINGTON, VIRGINIA**

LYNDON B. JOHNSON
36th President

Term — November 22, 1963
to January 20, 1969

Democratic Party

Birth: Stonewall, Texas. August 27, 1908
Zodiac Sign: Virgo
Ancestry: English - Irish, German, Scotch
Father: Samuel Ealy Johnson. Born: Buda, Texas, October 11, 1877. Died: Austin, Texas, October 22, 1937.
Mother: Rebekah Baines Johnson. Born: McKinney, Texas, June 26, 1881. Died: Austin, Texas, September 12, 1958.
Brother: Sam Houston (1914 - 1978).
Sisters: Rebekah Luruth (1910 - 1978). Josefa Hermine (1912 - 1961). Lucia Huffman (1916 -   ).
Wife: Claudia Alta Taylor. Born: Karnack, Texas, December 22, 1912.
Marriage: San Antonio. November 17, 1934.
Children: Lynda Bird (1944 -   ). Luci Baines (1947 -   ).
Education: Johnson City High School; Southwest Texas State Teachers College (B.S. 1930); Attended Georgetown University Law School.
Religion: Disciples of Christ
Occupation Before Presidency: Rancher; politician.
Pre-Presidential Offices: National Youth Administration Director in Texas; Member U.S. House of Representatives; Member U.S. Senate; Vice President of the U.S.
Military Service: Lt. Commander, Commander U.S. Naval Reserve (Active duty 1941 - 1942).
Age at Inauguration: 55
Note: The eighth Vice President who succeeded to the Presidency because of the death of his predecessor, John F. Kennedy.
First Administration
President: Lyndon B. Johnson
Inauguration: November 22, 1963
Aboard "Air Force One", Dallas, Texas

Election of 1964

Candidates	Electoral Vote
Lyndon B. Johnson (Democratic)	486
Barry M. Goldwater (Republican)	52

Second Administration
President: Lyndon B. Johnson
Vice President: Hubert H. Humphrey of Minnesota
Inauguration: January 20, 1965
The Capitol, Washington, D.C.
Occupation After Presidency: Retired to L.B.J. Ranch.
President at Time of Death: Richard M. Nixon
Death: Near Stonewall, Texas. January 22, 1973.
Cause of Death: Heart attack at age 65.
Place of Burial: Family cemetery, near Stonewall, Texas.

"If we fail now, then we will have forgotten in abundance what we learned in hardship; that democracy rests on faith; freedom asks more than it gives; and the judgement of God is harshest on those who are most favored."
— Inaugural Address, 1965

**LYNDON BAINES JOHNSON'S BIRTHPLACE
STONEWALL, TEXAS**

It was to this small farm house that Sam Ealy Johnson, Jr. brought his bride, the former Rebekah Baines, shortly after their marriage in August of 1907. It was also here that their first child, Lyndon, was born August 27, 1908.

The original house is no longer standing, but the present structure is almost an exact reconstruction of the early farmhouse. Its open hallway, or "dog-trot", provided ventilation in hot weather. It was built on the same location as the original Johnson home, using some stone and lumber from the old structure.

The Johnson family lived here from 1907 until 1913 when Lyndon was five years old.

Location:

Visitors Center just off U.S. 290. 14 miles west of Johnson City, Texas.

**• LYNDON B. JOHNSON'S BIRTHPLACE
STONEWALL, TEXAS**

**LYNDON B. JOHNSON'S SCHOOL
JUNCTION SCHOOL
STONEWALL, TEXAS**

Rebekah Baines Johnson was more than a bit worried about her little boy trekking over to the schoolhouse just to play with his cousins at recess. The teacher, "Miss Kate" Deadrich, already had her hands full with scholars of varying ages and grades in the little one room building which had first opened its doors in 1910. However, she was persuaded to take one more; and young Lyndon Baines Johnson began his formal education in 1912, at the tender age of four.

Fifty-three years later, on April 11, 1965, he returned here as President of the United States to sign the Elementary and Secondary Education Act, a bill he regarded as one of the most important of his administration. Appropriately, "Miss Kate" was at his side.

Location:

Visitors Center just off U.S. 290. 14 miles west of Johnson City, Texas.

LYNDON BAINES JOHNSON'S HOME
L.B.J. RANCH HOUSE
STONEWALL, TEXAS

The famed Texas White House was purchased by Lyndon B. Johnson in 1952. Built of native limestone and wood, it faces the scenic Pedernales River.

In 1972, President Johnson and Mrs. Lady Bird Johnson donated 200 acres of the ranch to the National Park Service, U.S. Department of the Interior. Mrs. Johnson continues to live there. The National Park Service conducts bus tours of the ranch at regular intervals every day.

Location:

Visitors Center just off U.S. Hwy. 290. 14 miles west of Johnson City, Texas.

LYNDON BAINES JOHNSON'S BOYHOOD HOME
JOHNSON CITY, TEXAS

Sam Ealy Johnson, Jr. purchased this comfortable house on 9th Street in late summer 1913, and moved the family from Stonewall, Texas. Lyndon had just turned five.

Besides the never-ending chores, Lyndon found time to do the things most kids did in Johnson City: breaking his arm falling out of the barn, playing first base or pitcher on sandlot and school teams, riding a borrowed donkey up to the Pedernales River, and occasionally getting into trouble.

He graduated from Johnson City High School in 1924 as President of the Senior Class.

Location:

On 9th Street, one block south of U.S. Hwy. 290 (Main Street), Johnson City, Texas.

LYNDON BAINES JOHNSON'S BURIAL SITE
STONEWALL, TEXAS

On January 25, 1973, Lyndon B. Johnson was buried as he wished, with simple ceremony, beneath the great live oaks in the family cemetery on the banks of the Pedernales River. The 36th President of the United States had come full-circle, from the farm house nearby, in which he was born to the White House, and back again.

Location:
Visitor Center just off U.S. 290. 14 miles west of Johnson City, Texas.

LYNDON BAINES JOHNSON LIBRARY
UNIVERSITY OF TEXAS
AUSTIN, TEXAS

"I hope that visitors who come here will achieve a closer understanding of the office of the Presidency, which affects their own lives so greatly. I hope that those who shared in the history of this time will remember it and see it in perspective, and that the young people who come here will get a clearer comprehension of what this nation tried to do in an eventful period of its history."

L.B.J.

Location:
University of Texas Campus. One block west of Interstate 35. (Take the Manor Road, Memorial Stadium exit of I-35). Austin, Texas.

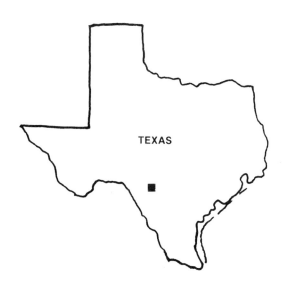

■ **LYNDON B. JOHNSON'S BURIAL SITE**
STONEWALL, TEXAS

139

RICHARD M. NIXON
37th President

**Term — January 20, 1969
to August 8, 1974**

Republican Party

Birth: Yorba Linda, California. January 9, 1913.

Zodiac Sign: Capricorn

Ancestry: Welsh, Scottish, Irish, English

Father: Francis Anthony Nixon. Born: Elk Township, Vinton County, Ohio, December 3, 1878. Died: La Habra, California, September 4, 1956.

Mother: Hannah Milhous Nixon. Born: Near Butlerville, Jinnings County, Indiana, March 7, 1885. Died: Whittier, California, September 30, 1967.

Brothers: Harold Samuel (1909 - 1933). Francis Donald (1914 -   ). Arthur (1918 - 1925). Edward (1930 -   ).

Wife: Thelma Catherine Ryan. Born: Ely, Nevada, March 16, 1912.

Marriage: Riverside, California. June 21, 1940.

Children: Patricia (1946 -   ). Julie (1948 -   ).

Education: Whittier High School; Whittier College, Whittier, California, graduated (1934); L.L.B. Duke University Law School, Durham, North Carolina, graduated (1937).

Religion: Society of Friends (Quaker)

Occupation Before Presidency: Lawyer

Pre-Presidential Offices: Member of the House of Representatives; Member of U.S. Senate; Vice President of the U.S.

Military Service: Lieutenant (J.G.); Lieutenant Commander, U.S. Navy; Commander U.S. Naval Reserve (active duty, 1942 - 1946).

Political Party: Republican

Age at Inauguration: 56

Election of 1968

Candidates	Electoral Vote
Richard M. Nixon (Republican)	301
Hubert H. Humphrey (Democratic)	191
George C. Wallace (Independent)	46

First Administration
President: Richard M. Nixon
Vice President: Spiro T. Agnew of Maryland
Inauguration: January 20, 1969
The Capitol, Washington, D.C.

Election of 1972

Candidates	Electoral Vote
Richard M. Nixon (Republican)	521
George S. McGovern (Democratic)	17

Second Administration
President: Richard M. Nixon
Vice President: Spiro T. Agnew of Maryland
Agnew resigned October 10, 1973
Second Vice President: Gerald R. Ford of Michigan
December 6, 1973
Inauguration: January 20, 1973
The Capitol, Washington, D.C.
Nixon resigned August 9, 1974.

Occupation After Presidency: Retired; writing his memoirs.

"The peace we seek to win is not victory over any other people, but the peace that comes "with healing in its wings"; with compassion for those who have suffered; with understanding for those who have opposed us; with the opportunity for all the peoples of this earth to choose their own destiny."

— Inaugural Address, 1969

**RICHARD M. NIXON'S BIRTHPLACE
YORBA LINDA, CALIFORNIA**

**RICHARD M. NIXON'S BIRTHPLACE
YORBA LINDA, CALIFORNIA**

Richard Nixon was born in Yorba Linda, California on January 9, 1913, second of five sons of Francis Anthony and Hannah Milhous Nixon. Francis Anthony Nixon ran a citrus farm in Yorba Linda and, later a combination grocery store and gasoline station in Whittier, California.
Location:
    18161 Yorba Linda Blvd., Yorba Linda, California.

**RICHARD M. NIXON'S BIRTHPLACE
YORBA LINDA, CALIFORNIA**

**• RICHARD M. NIXON'S BIRTHPLACE
YORBA LINDA, CALIFORNIA**

**RICHARD M. NIXON'S HOME
SAN CLEMENTE, CALIFORNIA**

With panoramic views of the Pacific Ocean on one side and Orange County's towering hills on the other, the lovely La Casa Pacifica stands amid 3½ well landscaped acres at Cypress Shores, San Clemente's southern boundary. A fountain is in the open patio, surrounded by the beautifully decorated red tile and stucco Spanish style home.

Location:

Del Presidente Avenue off Interstate 5, San Clemente, California. Private—not open to the public.

Other Homes:

Key Biscayne, Florida.

GERALD R. FORD
38th President

**Term — August 9, 1974
to January 20, 1977**

Republican Party

Gerald R. Ford

Birth: Omaha, Nebraska. July 14, 1913.
Zodiac Sign: Cancer.
Father: Leslie King. Born: Chadron, Nebraska, July 25, 1881. Died: Tuscon, Arizona, February 18, 1941.
Step Father: Gerald R. Ford, Sr. Born: 1890. Died: 1962. Mother's second husband who legally adopted her son in 1935, when his name was changed from Leslie King to Gerald R. Ford.
Mother: Dorothy Gardner King. Born: Harvard, Illinois, February 27, 1892. Died: Grand Rapids, Michigan, September 17, 1967.
Half Siblings: Father's side: Majorie King (1921 -). Leslie King (1923 -). Patricia King (1925 -).
Half Siblings: Mother's side: Thomas Ford (1918 -). Richard Ford (1924 -). James Ford (1927 -).
Wife: Elizabeth Bloomer. Born: Chicago, Illinois, April 8, 1918.
Marriage: Grace Episcopal Church, Grand Rapids, Michigan. October 15, 1948.
Children: Michael Gerald (1950 -). John Gardner (1952 -). Steven Meigs (1956 -). Susan Elizabeth (1957 -).
Education: South High School, Grand Rapids, Michigan; University of Michigan B.A. (1935); Yale University Law School L.L.B. (1941).
Religion: Episcopalian
Occupation Before Presidency: Lawyer
Military Service: Lieutenant Commander, U.S. Navy (active duty 1942 - 1946).
Pre-Presidential Offices: Member U.S. House of Representatives; Minority Leader, House of Representatives; Vice President of the U.S.
Political Party: Republican
Age at Inauguration: 61

Note: The first President who succeeded to the Presidency because of the resignation of his predecessor, Richard M. Nixon.
The Ford Administration
President: Gerald R. Ford
Vice President: Nelson Rockefeller of New York. December 19, 1974
Inauguration: August 9, 1974
The Capitol, Washington, D.C.
Occupation After Presidency: Writing his memoirs; lecturing at colleges and universities.

"You have not elected me as your President, by your ballots, and so I ask you to confirm me as your President with your prayers. I have not sought this enormous responsibility, but I will not shirk it — 'My fellow Americans, our long national nightmare is over', our Constitution works, our great republic is a government of laws and not of men. Here the people rule. God helping me, I will not let you down.

— Inaugural Address, 1974

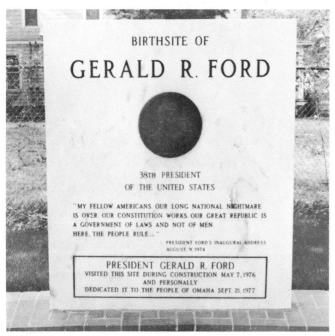

GERALD R. FORD'S BIRTHPLACE
OMAHA, NEBRASKA

GERALD R. FORD MUSEUM
GRAND RAPIDS, MICHIGAN

Gerald R. Ford Museum is located on the west bank of the Grand River in President Ford's hometown. The Ford Museum traces the story of his life and public service from his childhood in Grand Rapids to the White House. Dedicated on September 18, 1981, the museum was built by the Gerald R. Ford Commemorative Committee and is administered by the National Archives and Record Service of the General Service Administration.
Location:
303 Pearl St. N.W., Grand Rapids, Michigan.

GERALD R. FORD'S BIRTHPLACE
OMAHA, NEBRASKA

Gerald R. Ford, 38th President of the United States, was born in Omaha, Nebraska, July 14, 1913.

The design includes a replica of the cupola of President Ford's early home and contains information about the birthplace along with personal comments of the President. The memorial includes a large flagpole and a fountain near the colonade.
Location:
32nd and Woolworth Avenues, Omaha, Nebraska.

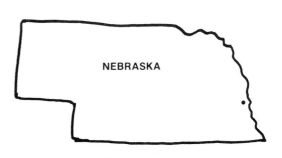

NEBRASKA

• GERALD R. FORD'S BIRTHPLACE
OMAHA, NEBRASKA

144

GERALD R. FORD LIBRARY
NORTH CAMPUS, UNIVERSITY OF MICHIGAN
ANN ARBOR, MICHIGAN

The Gerald R. Ford Library on the North Campus of the University of Michigan, Ann Arbor. The Ford Library houses the papers and other historical materials of Gerald Ford's service as Congressman, Vice President and President of the United States.

Location:
North Campus, University of Michigan. 1000 Beal Avenue, Ann Arbor, Michigan.

GERALD R. FORD'S HOME
THUNDERBIRD COUNTRY CLUB
RANCHO MIRAGE, CALIFORNIA

Gerald R. Ford's home faces the 13th fairway on Thunderbird Country Club.

Private — Not open to the public.

Location:
Thunderbird Country Club, Rancho Mirage, California

JAMES CARTER
39th President

[signature: Jimmy Carter]

Term — January 20, 1977 to January 20 1981

Democratic Party

Birth: Plains, Georgia. October 1, 1924.

Zodiac Sign: Libra.

Father: James Earl Carter. Born: September 12, 1894. Died: July 22, 1953.

Mother: Lillian Gordy Carter. Born: Richland, Georgia, August 15, 1898.

Brother: William Alton Carter III (Billy) (1937 -   ).

Sisters: Gloria (Mrs. Walter G. Spann). Ruth (Mrs. Robert T. Stapleton).

Wife: Rosalynn Smith. Born: Plains, Georgia, August 18, 1927.

Married: Plains, Georgia. July 7, 1946.

Children: John William (Jack) (1947 -   ). James Earl III (Chip) (1950 -   ). Donnel Jeffrey (1952 -   ). Amy Lynn (1967 -   ).

Education: Georgia Southwestern College. U.S. Naval Academy graduate (1947). Did graduate work in nuclear physics in Union College.

Religion: Baptist

Occupation Before Presidency: Farmer, warehouseman, businessman.

Military Service: Lieutenant Commander, U.S. Navy (1946-1953).

Pre-Presidential Offices: Georgia State Senator 1962 - 1966; Governor of Georgia 1971 - 1974.

Political Party: Democratic

Age at Inauguration: 52

Election of 1976

Candidates	Electoral Vote
James E. Carter (Democratic)	297
Gerald R. Ford (Republican)	241

The Carter Administration

President: James E. Carter

Vice President: Walter F. Mondale of Minnesota

Inauguration: January 20, 1977

The Capitol, Washington, D.C.

Occupation After Presidency: Lecturing at colleges and universities; writing his memoirs.

"Two centuries ago, our Nation's birth was a milestone in the long quest for freedom, but the bold and brilliant dream which excited the founders of our nation still awaits its consummation, I have no new dream to set forth, but rather urge a fresh faith in the old dream."

— Inaugural Address, 1977

JAMES EARL CARTER'S BIRTHPLACE
PLAINS, GEORGIA

James Earl Carter, Jr. was born October 1, 1924 in the Wise Sanitarium (Convalescent Home), Plains, Georgia. The Wise Sanitarium was revered by many as the "Mayo Clinic" of the South.

Location:

Hospital Street, Plains, Georgia.

JAMES EARL CARTER'S BOYHOOD HOME
ARCHERY, GEORGIA

Jimmy Carter was approaching his fourth birthday before his father could afford to buy a house for his family.

This cottage about three miles west of Plains, near the railroad flag stop known as Archery, would be Jimmy's home through the rest of his boyhood

Location:

2 miles west of Plains, Georgia on Hwy. 280 and Ga. 27. Plains, Georgia.

GEORGIA

• JAMES EARL CARTER'S BIRTHPLACE
PLAINS, GEORGIA

147

JAMES EARL CARTER'S CHURCH
PLAINS BAPTIST CHURCH
PLAINS, GEORGIA

"My religion means more to me than anything else in the world." A Baptist, James Carter taught Sunday school, and before he started running for the Presidency, he toured the New England states with his church group.
Location:
    Bond Street and Paschal Street, Plains, Georgia.

JAMES EARL CARTER'S MOTHER'S HOME
MISS LILLIAN'S HOME
PLAINS, GEORGIA

Private — Not open to the public.
Location:
    Church Street, Plains, Georgia.

148

UNITED METHODIST CHURCH
MARRIAGE PLACE OF JIMMY CARTER AND ROSALYNN SMITH
PLAINS, GEORGIA

Jimmy Carter and Rosalynn Smith were married July 7, 1946, in the Plains Methodist Church. Jimmy Carter, an ensign in the United States Navy was almost twenty-two, and Rosalynn was six weeks short of her nineteenth birthday.

Shortly after their marriage, Jimmy and Rosalynn settled into a tiny apartment in Norfolk, Virginia.

Location:
Church Street, Plains, Georgia.

ROSALYNN SMITH CARTER'S GIRLHOOD HOME
MRS. ALLIE SMITH'S HOME
PLAINS, GEORGIA

Rosalynn's family, the Smith's, did not match the Carter's either in economic or social status. Rosalynn's father, Edgar, was the town mechanic, earning barely enough to support his family, especially during the Depression when his wife, Allie, had to supplement their meager income by utilizing her skills as a seamstress.

Early one Sunday morning in 1940, Edgar Smith summoned his wife, Allie, and their four children to his bedroom and told them he was dying of leukemia. To their astonishment, he also said he had scrimped and saved, and managed to put away some money for his children to further their education. He wanted them all to go to college. "I want you to do better in life than I have", he told them.

Edgar Smith died that fall, when Rosalynn was thirteen.

After graduation from Plains High School in the spring of 1944, Rosalynn fulfilled at least part of her father's dying wishes by enrolling in a secretarial course at Georgia Southwestern, a junior college in Americus, a few miles away from Plains.

Private — Not open to the public.
Location:
Bond Street, Plains, Georgia.

JAMES EARL CARTER'S HOME
PLAINS, GEORGIA

Jimmy Carter and his wife Rosalynn continue to live in this home in Plains, Georgia.

Private — Not open to the public.

Location:

Woodlawn Drive, Plains, Georgia.

RONALD REAGAN
40th President

Term — January 20, 1981

Republican Party

Ronald Reagan

Birth: Tampico, Illinois. February 6, 1911.

Zodiac Sign: Aquarius.

Father: John Edward Reagan. Born: Bennett, Iowa, July 13, 1883. Died: Hollywood, California, 1941.

Mother: Nelle Wilson Reagan. Born: Fulton, Illinois, July 24, 1883. Died: 1962.

Brother: John Neil (1908 -   ).

First Wife: Jane Wyman. Born: St. Joseph, Missouri, January 4, 1914.

First Marriage: Glendale, California. January 26, 1940. Divorced in 1948.

Children: Maureen (1941 -   ). Michael (adopted) (1945 -   ).

Second Wife: Nancy Davis. Born: Manhattan, New York, July 6, 1923 — "Anne Frances Robbins". She became the adopted daughter of Dr. Loyal Davis as soon as her fourteenth birthday made it legally possible.

Second Marriage: North Hollywood, California. March 4, 1952.

Children: Patricia (1952 -   ). Ronald, Jr. (1958 -   ).

Education: Eureka College, Eureka, Illinois. (graduated 1932).

Religion: Christian Church

Occupation Before Presidency: Sports broadcaster; actor; businessman; rancher; U.S.A.F. active duty 1942-1945).

Military Service: Army Air Corps during World War II.

Pre-Presidential Offices: Governor of California 1967 - 1975).

Political Party: Republican

Age at Inauguration: 69

Election of 1980

Candidates	Electoral Vote
Ronald Wilson Reagan (Republican)	489
James Earl Carter (Democratic)	49

First Administration

President: Ronald Wilson Reagan
Vice President: George Bush of Texas
Inauguration: January 20, 1981
The Capitol, Washington, D.C.

Election of 1984

Candidates	Electoral Vote
Ronald Wilson Reagan (Republican)	525
Walter Mondale (Democrat)	13

Second Administration

President: Ronald Wilson Reagan
Vice President: George Bush of Texas
Inauguration: January 21, 1985
The Capitol, Washington, D.C.

Ronald Reagan described his followers in the November 1980 Saturday Evening Post as:
"...people who get up every day and go to work, look after their children, support their churches, and schools, believe in standards of right and wrong and ask nothing more of government than simply to be kept safe in their homes."

RONALD REAGAN'S BIRTHPLACE
TAMPICO, ILLINOIS

Ronald W. Reagan was born February 6, 1911 in a five room apartment above a bakery in Tampico, a small town in rural northwestern Illinois. He was the youngest of two sons born to John Edward and Nelle Wilson Reagan. John was an Irish-Catholic Democrat who had a number of jobs in his lifetime. Nelle, of Scotch-English descent, was a pious Protestant and natural do-gooder who instilled her love for the theater into her son Ronald.
Location:
111 Main Street, Tampico, Illinois.

ILLINOIS

• RONALD REAGAN'S BIRTHPLACE
TAMPICO, ILLINOIS

RONALD REAGAN'S BOYHOOD HOME
DIXON, ILLINOIS

RONALD REAGAN'S BOYHOOD HOME
DIXON, ILLINOIS

In 1921, John Reagan and his family moved to Dixon, Illinois.

President Reagan graduated from North Dixon High School in 1928, having served as student body president. To save money for his college education, President Reagan worked in the summer on a construction job for sixty hours each week and worked fifteen more hours each week as a lifeguard on the Rock River, which flows through downtown Dixon, Illinois. President Reagan remained in Dixon until he was 21 years old.

Location:

816 South Hennepin, Dixon, Illinois.

Other Homes

Ronald W. Reagan's Home
1669 San Onofre Drive
Pacific Palisides, California

Private — Not open to the public.

Ronald W. Reagan's Ranch
Rancho del Cielo
(Sky Ranch)
Refugio Canyon
Santa Barbara, California

Private — Not open to the public.